Idylls of the Bible

AMS PRESS

NEW YORK

Frances E. W. Harper.

Idylls of the Bible

...BY...

MRS. F. E. W. HARPER

PHILADELPHIA

1006 BAINBRIDGE STREET

1901

Library of Congress Cataloging in Publication Data

Harper, Frances Ellen Watkins, 1825-1911.
   Idylls of the Bible.

   Poems.
   Reprint of the 1901 ed. published in Philadelphia.
   1. Christian poetry, American.   I. Title.
PS1799.H7I3   1975   811'.3   75-168245
ISBN 0-404-00058-4

From the edition of 1901, Philadelphia
First AMS edition published in 1975

Manufactured in the United States of America

AMS PRESS INC.
NEW YORK, N. Y. 10003

MOSES·

A STORY OF THE NILE

THE PARTING.—Chapter I.

MOSES.

Kind and gracious princess, more than friend,
I've come to thank thee for thy goodness,
And to breathe into thy generous ears
My last and sad farewell. I go to join
The fortunes of my race, and to put aside
All other bright advantages, save
The approval of my conscience and the meed
Of rightly doing.

PRINCESS.

What means, my son, this strange election?
What wild chimera floats across thy mind?
What sudden impulse moves thy soul? Thou who
Hast only trod the court of kings, why seek
Instead the paths of labor? Thou, whose limbs
Have known no other garb than that which well
Befits our kingly state, why rather choose
The badge of servitude and toil?

MOSES.

Let me tell thee, gracious princess; 'tis no
Sudden freak nor impulse wild that moves my mind.
I feel an earnest purpose binding all
My soul unto a strong resolve, which bids
Me put aside all other ends and aims,
Until the hour shall come when God—the God
Our fathers loved and worshipped—shall break our
    chains,
And lead our willing feet to freedom.

PRINCESS.

Listen to me, Moses: thou art young,
And the warm blood of youth flushes thy veins
Like generous wine; thou wearest thy manhood
Like a crown; but what king e'er cast
His diadem in the dust, to be trampled
Down by every careless foot? Thou hast
Bright dreams and glowing hopes; could'st thou not
    live
Them out as well beneath the radiance
Of our throne as in the shadow of those
Bondage-darkened huts?

MOSES.

Within those darkened huts my mother plies her tasks,
My father bends to unrequited toil;
And bitter tears moisten the bread my brethren eat.
And when I gaze upon their cruel wrongs

The very purple on my limbs seems drenched
With blood, the warm blood of my own kindred
    race ;
And then thy richest viands pall upon my taste,
And discord jars in every tone of song.
I cannot live in pleasure while they faint
In pain.

PRINCESS.

How like a dream the past floats back: it seems
But yesterday when I lay tossing upon
My couch of pain, a torpor creeping through
Each nerve, a fever coursing through my veins.
And there I lay, dreaming of lilies fair,
Of lotus flowers and past delights, and all
The bright, glad hopes, that give to early life
Its glow and flush ; and thus day after day
Dragged its slow length along, until, one morn,
The breath of lilies, fainting on the air,
Floated into my room, and then I longed once more
To gaze upon the Nile, as on the face
Of a familiar friend, whose absence long
Had made a mournful void within the heart.
I summoned to my side my maids, and bade
Them place my sandals on my feet, and lead
Me to the Nile, where I might bathe my weary
Limbs within the cooling flood, and gather
Healing from the sacred stream.
I sought my favorite haunt, and, bathing, found
New tides of vigor coursing through my veins.

Refreshed, I sat me down to weave a crown of lotus
    leaves
And lilies fair, and while I sat in a sweet
Revery, dreaming of life and hope, I saw
A little wicker-basket hidden among
The flags and lilies of the Nile, and I called
My maidens and said, " Nillias and Osiria
Bring me that little ark which floats beside
The stream." They ran and brought me a precious
    burden.
'Twas an ark woven with rushes and daubed
With slime, and in it lay a sleeping child ;
His little hand amid his clustering curls,
And a bright flush upon his glowing cheek.
He wakened with a smile, and reached out his hand
To meet the welcome of the mother's kiss,
When strange faces met his gaze, and he drew back
With a grieved, wondering look, while disappoint
    ment
Shook the quivering lip that missed the mother's
Wonted kiss, and the babe lifted his voice and wept.
Then my heart yearned towards him, and I resolved
That I would brave my father's wrath and save
The child ; but while I stood gazing upon
His wondrous beauty, I saw beside me
A Hebrew girl, her eyes bent on me
With an eager, questioning look, and drawing
Near, she timidly said, " shall I call a nurse ?'
I bade her go ; she soon returned, and with her

Came a woman of the Hebrew race, whose
Sad, sweet, serious eyes seemed overflowing
With a strange and sudden joy. I placed the babe
Within her arms and said, " Nurse this child for
    me ;"
And the babe nestled there like one at home,
While o'er the dimples of his face rippled
The brightest, sweetest smiles, and I was well
Content to leave him in her care ; and well
Did she perform her part. When many days had
Passed she brought the child unto the palace ;
And one morning, while I sat toying with
His curls and listening to the prattle of his
Untrained lips, my father, proud and stately,
Saw me bending o'er the child and said,
" Charmian, whose child is this ? who of my lords
Calls himself father to this goodly child ?
He surely must be a happy man."
       Then I said, " Father, he is mine. He is a
Hebrew child that I have saved from death." He
Suddenly recoiled, as if an adder
Had stung him, and said, " Charmian, take that
Child hence. How darest thou bring a member
Of that mean and servile race within my doors ?
Nay, rather let me send for Nechos, whose
Ready sword shall rid me of his hateful presence."
Then kneeling at his feet, and catching
Hold of his royal robes, I said, " Not so,
Oh ! honored father, he is mine ; I snatched

Him from the hungry jaws of death, and foiled
The greedy crocodile of his prey ; he has
Eaten bread within thy palace walls, and thy
Salt lies upon his fresh young lips ; he has
A claim upon thy mercy."

         " Charmian, ' ne said
" I have decreed that every man child of that
Hated race shall die. The oracles have said
The pyramids shall wane before their shadow,
And from them a star shall rise whose light shall
Spread over earth a baleful glow ; and this is why
I root them from the land ; their strength is weakness
To my throne. I shut them from the light lest they
Bring darkness to my kingdom. Now, Charmian,
Give me up the child, and let him die."
Then clasping the child closer to my heart,
I said, " the pathway to his life is through my own ;
Around that life I throw my heart, a wall
Of living, loving clay." Dark as the thunder
Clouds of distant lands became my father's brow.
And his eyes flashed with the fierce lightnings
Of his wrath ; but while I plead, with eager
Eyes upturned, I saw a sudden change come
Over him ; his eyes beamed with unwonted
Tenderness, and he said, " Charmian, arise,
Thy prayer is granted ; just then thy dead mother
Came to thine eyes, and the light of Asenath
Broke over thy face. Asenath was the light
Of my home ; the star that faded out too

Suddenly from my dwelling, and left my life
To darkness, grief and pain, and for her sake,
Not thine, I'll spare the child." And thus I saved
Thee twice—once from the angry sword and once
From the devouring flood. Moses, thou art
Doubly mine; as such I claimed thee then, as such
I claim thee now. I've nursed no other child
Upon my knee, and pressed upon no other
Lips the sweetest kisses of my love, and now,
With rash and careless hand, thou dost thrust aside
    that love.
There was a painful silence, a silence
So hushed and still that you might have almost
Heard the hurried breathing of one and the quick
Throbbing of the other's heart : for Moses,
He was slow of speech, but she was eloquent
With words of tenderness and love, and had breathed
Her full heart into her lips ; but there was
Firmness in the young man's choice, and he beat
    back
The opposition of her lips with the calm
Grandeur of his will, and again he essayed to speak.

MOSES.

Gracious lady, thou remembrest well
The Hebrew nurse to whom thou gavest thy found
    ling.
That woman was my mother ; from her lips I
Learned the grand traditions of our race that float.

With all their weird and solemn beauty, around
Our wrecked and blighted fortunes. How oft!
With kindling eye and glowing cheek, forgetful
Of the present pain, she would lead us through
The distant past: the past, hallowed by deeds
Of holy faith and lofty sacrifice.
How she would tell us of Abraham,
The father of our race, that he dwelt in Ur;
Of the Chaldees, and when the Chaldean king
Had called him to his sacrifice, that he
Had turned from his dumb idols to the living
God, and wandered out from kindred, home and
    race,
Led by his faith in God alone; and she would
Tell us,—(we were three,) my brother Aaron,
The Hebrew girl thou sentest to call a nurse,
And I, her last, her loved and precious child;
She would tell us that one day our father
Abraham heard a voice, bidding him offer
Up in sacrifice the only son of his
Beautiful and beloved Sarah; that the father's
Heart shrank not before the bitter test of faith,
But he resolved to give his son to God
As a burnt offering upon Moriah's mount;
That the uplifted knife glittered in the morning
Sun, when, sweeter than the music of a thousand
Harps, he heard a voice bidding him stay his hand,
And spare the child; and how his faith, like gold
Tried in the fiercest fire, shone brighter through

Its fearful test. And then she would tell us
Of a promise, handed down from sire to son,
That God, the God our fathers loved and worshiped,
Would break our chains, and bring to us a great
Deliverance; that we should dwell in peace
Beneath our vines and palms, our flocks and herds
Increase, and joyful children crowd our streets;
And then she would lift her eyes unto the far
Off hills and tell us of the patriarchs
Of our line, who sleep in distant graves within
That promised land; and now I feel the hour
Draws near which brings deliverance to our race.

PRINCESS.

These are but the dreams of thy young fancy;
I cannot comprehend thy choice. I have heard
Of men who have waded through slaughter
To a throne; of proud ambitions, struggles
Fierce and wild for some imagined good; of men
Who have even cut in twain the crimson threads
That lay between them and a throne; but I
Never heard of men resigning ease for toil,
The splendor of a palace for the squalor
Of a hut, and casting down a diadem
To wear a servile badge.
               Sadly she gazed
Upon the fair young face lit with its lofty
Faith and high resolves—the dark prophetic eyes
Which seemed to look beyond the present pain

Unto the future greatness of his race.
As she stood before him in the warm
Loveliness of her ripened womanhood,
Her languid eyes glowed with unwonted fire,
And the bright tropical blood sent its quick
Flushes o'er the olive of her cheek, on which
Still lay the lingering roses of her girlhood.
Grief, wonder, and surprise flickered like shadows
O'er her face as she stood slowly crushing
With unconscious hand the golden tassels
Of her crimson robe. She had known life only
By its brightness, and could not comprehend
The grandeur of the young man's choice; but she
Felt her admiration glow before the earnest
Faith that tore their lives apart and led him
To another destiny. She had hoped to see
The crown of Egypt on his brow, the sacred
Leopard skin adorn his shoulders, and his seat
The throne of the proud Pharaoh's; but now her
Dream had faded out and left a bitter pang
Of anguish in its stead. And thus they parted,
She to brood in silence o'er her pain, and he
To take his mission from the hands of God
And lead his captive race to freedom.
With silent lips but aching heart she bowed
Her queenly head and let him pass, and he
Went forth to share the fortune of his race,
Esteeming that as better far than pleasures
Bought by sin and gilded o'er with vice.

And he had chosen well, for on his brow
God poured the chrism of a holy work.
And thus anointed he has stood a bright
Ensample through the changing centuries of time

Chapter II.

It was a great change from the splendor, light
And pleasure of a palace to the lowly huts
Of those who sighed because of cruel bondage.
                              As he passed
Into the outer courts of that proud palace,
He paused a moment just to gaze upon
The scenes 'mid which his early life had passed—
The pleasant haunts amid the fairest flowers,—
The fountains tossing on the air their silver spray,—
The statues breathing music soft and low
To greet the first faint flushes of the morn,—
The obelisks that rose in lofty grandeur
From their stony beds—the sphynxes gaunt and
     grim,
With unsolved riddles on their lips—and all
The bright creation's painters art and sculptors
Skill had gathered in those regal halls, where mirth
And dance, and revelry, and song had chased
With careless feet the bright and fleeting hours.

He was leaving all ; but no regrets came
Like a shadow o'er his mind, for he had felt
The quickening of a higher life, as if his
Soul had wings and he were conscious of their growth
And yet there was a tender light in those
Dark eyes which looked their parting on the scenes
Of beauty, where his life had been a joyous
Dream enchanted with delight; but he trampled
On each vain regret as on a vanquished foe,
And went forth a strong man, girded with lofty
Purposes and earnest faith. He journeyed on
Till palaces and domes and lofty fanes,
And gorgeous temples faded from his sight,
And the lowly homes of Goshen came in view.
There he saw the women of his race kneading
Their tale of bricks ; the sons of Abraham
Crouching beneath their heavy burdens. He saw
The increasing pallor on his sisters cheek,
The deepening shadows on his mother's brow,
The restless light that glowed in Aaron's eye,
As if a hidden fire were smouldering
In his brain ; and bending o'er his mother
In a tender, loving way, he said, " Mother,
I've come to share the fortunes of my race,—
To dwell within these lowly huts,—to wear
The badge of servitude and toil, and eat
The bitter bread of penury and pain."
A sudden light beamed from his mother's eye,
And she said, " How's this, my son ? but yesterday

Two Hebrews, journeying from On to Goshen,
Told us they had passed the temple of the Sun
But dared not enter, only they had heard
That it was a great day in On; that thou hadst
Forsworn thy kindred, tribe and race; hadst bowed
Thy knee to Egypt's vain and heathen worship
Hadst denied the God of Abraham, of Isaac,
And of Jacob, and from henceforth wouldst
Be engrafted in Pharaoh's regal line,
And be called the son of Pharaoh's daughter.
When thy father Amram heard the cruel news
He bowed his head upon his staff and wept.
But I had stronger faith than that.   By faith
I hid thee when the bloody hands of Pharaoh
Were searching 'mid our quivering heart strings
Dooming our sons to death; by faith I wove
The rushes of thine ark and laid thee 'mid
The flags and lilies of the Nile, and saw
The answer to that faith when Pharaoh's daughter
Placed thee in my arms, and bade me nurse the
    child
For her; and by that faith sustained, I heard
As idle words the cruel news that stabbed
Thy father like a sword."
" The Hebrews did not hear aright; last week
There was a great day in On, from Esoan's gate
Unto the mighty sea; the princes, lords
And chamberlains of Egypt were assembled;
The temple of the sun was opened.   Isis

And Osiris were unveiled before the people,
Apis and Orus were crowned with flowers;
Golden censers breathed their fragrance on the air;
The sacrifice was smoking on the altar;
The first fruits of the Nile lay on the tables
Of the sun: the music rose in lofty swells,
Then sank in cadences so soft and low
Till all the air grew tremulous with rapture.
The priests of On were there, with sacred palms
Within their hands and lotus leaves upon their
Brows; Pharaoh and his daughter sat waiting
In their regal chairs; all were ready to hear
Me bind my soul to Egypt, and to swear
Allegiance to her gods. The priests of On
Drew near to lay their hands upon my head
And bid me swear, 'Now, by Osiris, judge
Of all the dead, and Isis, mother of us
All,' that henceforth I'd forswear my kindred,
Tribe and race; would have no other gods
Than those of Egypt; would be engrafted
Into Pharaoh's royal line, and be called
The son of Pharaoh's daughter. Then, mother
Dear, I lived the past again. Again I sat
Beside thee, my lips apart with childish
Wonder, my eager eyes uplifted to thy
Glowing face, and my young soul gathering
Inspiration from thy words. Again I heard
Thee tell the grand traditions of our race,
The blessed hopes and glorious promises

That weave their golden threads among the sombre
Tissues of our lives, and shimmer still amid
The gloom and shadows of our lot. Again
I heard thee tell of Abraham, with his constant
Faith and earnest trust in God, unto whom
The promise came that in his seed should all
The nations of the earth be blessed. Of Isaac
Blessing with disappointed lips his first born son,
From whom the birthright had departed. Of Jacob,
With his warm affections and his devious ways,
Flying berore the wrath of Esau ; how he
Slumbered in the wild, and saw amid his dreams
A ladder reaching to the sky, on which God's
Angels did descend, and waking, with a solemn
Awe o'ershadowing all, his soul exclaimed, 'How
Dreadful is this place. Lo! God is here, and I
Knew it not.' Of Joseph, once a mighty prince
Within this land, who shrank in holy horror
From the soft white hand that beckoned him to sin
Whose heart, amid the pleasures, pomp and pride
Of Egypt, was ever faithful to his race,
And when his life was trembling on its frailest chord
He turned his dying eyes to Canaan, and made
His brethren swear that they would make his grave
Among the patriarchs of his line, because
 Machpelah's cave, where Abraham bowed before
The sons of Heth, and bought a place to lay
His loved and cherished dead, was dearer to his
Dying heart than the proudest tomb amid
The princely dead of Egypt.

Then, like the angels, mother dear, who met
Our father Jacob on his way, thy words
Came back as messengers of light to guide
My steps, and I refused to be called the son
Of Pharaoh's daughter. I saw the priests of On
Grow pale with fear, an ashen terror creeping
O'er the princess' face, while Pharaoh's brow grew
Darker than the purple of his cloak. But I
Endured, as seeing him who hides his face
Behind the brightness of his glory.
And thus I left the pomp and pride of Egypt
To cast my lot among the people of my race."

FLIGHT INTO MIDIAN.—Chapter III

The love of Moses for his race soon found
A stern expression. Pharaoh was building
A pyramid; ambitious, cold and proud,
He scrupled not at means to gain his ends.
When he feared the growing power of Israel
He stained his hands in children's blood, and held
A carnival of death in Goshen; but now
He wished to hand his name and memory
Down unto the distant ages, and instead
Of lading that memory with the precious
Fragrance of the kindest deeds and words, he

Essayed to write it out in stone, as cold
And hard, and heartless as himself.

                        And Israel was
The fated race to whom the cruel tasks
Were given.   Day after day a cry of wrong
And anguish, some dark deed of woe and crime,
Came to the ear of Moses, and he said,
" These reports are ever harrowing my soul;
I will go unto the fields where Pharaoh's
Officers exact their labors, and see
If these things be so—if they smite the feeble
At their tasks, and goad the aged on to toils
Beyond their strength—if neither age nor sex
Is spared the cruel smiting of their rods."
And Moses went to see his brethren.

                       'Twas eventide,
And the laborers were wending their way
Unto their lowly huts.   'Twas a sad sight,—
The young girls walked without the bounding steps
Of youth, with faces prematurely old,
As if the rosy hopes and sunny promises
Of life had never flushed their cheeks with girlish
Joy; and there were men whose faces seemed to say
We bear our lot in hopeless pain, we've bent unto
Our burdens until our shoulders fit them,
And as slaves we crouch beneath our servitude
And toil.   But there were men whose souls were cast
In firmer moulds, men with dark secretive eyes,
Which seemed to say, to day we bide our time,

And hide our wrath in every nerve, and only
Wait a fitting hour to strike the hands that press
Us down. Then came the officers of Pharaoh;
They trod as lords, their faces flushed with pride
And insolence, watching the laborers
Sadly wending their way from toil to rest.
And Moses' heart swelled with a mighty pain; sadly
Musing, he sought a path that led him
From the busy haunts of men. But even there
The cruel wrong trod in his footsteps; he heard
A heavy groan, then harsh and bitter words,
And, looking back, he saw an officer
Of Pharaoh smiting with rough and cruel hand
An aged man. Then Moses' wrath o'erflowed
His lips, and every nerve did tremble
With a sense of wrong, and bounding forth he
Cried unto the smiter, " Stay thy hand; seest thou
That aged man? His head is whiter than our
Desert sands; his limbs refuse to do thy
Bidding because thy cruel tasks have drained
Away their strength." The Egyptian raised his eyes
With sudden wonder; who was this that dared
    dispute
His power? Only a Hebrew youth. His
Proud lip curved in scornful anger, and he
Waved a menace with his hand, saying, " back
To thy task base slave, nor dare resist the will
Of Pharaoh." Then Moses' wrath o'erleaped the
    bounds

Of prudence, and with a heavy blow he felled
The smiter to the earth, and Israel had
One tyrant less. Moses saw the mortal paleness
Chase the flushes from the Egyptian's face,
The whitening lips that breathed no more defiance
And the relaxing tension of the well knit limbs;
And when he knew that he was dead, he hid
Him in the sand and left him to his rest.
                    Another day Moses walked
Abroad, and saw two brethren striving
For mastery; and then his heart grew full
Of tender pity. They were brethren, sharers
Of a common wrong: should not their wrongs more
Closely bind their hearts, and union, not division,
Be their strength? And feeling thus, he said, "ye
Are brethren, wherefore do ye strive together?'
But they threw back his words in angry tones
And asked if he had come to judge them, and would
Mete to them the fate of the Egyptian ?
Then Moses knew the sand had failed to keep
His secret, that his life no more was safe
In Goshen, and he fled unto the deserts
Of Arabia and became a shepherd
For the priest of Midian.

Chapter IV.

Men grow strong in action, but in solitude
Their thoughts are ripened. Like one who cuts away
The bridge on which he has walked in safety
To the other side, so Moses cut off all retreat
To Pharaoh's throne, and did choose the calling
Most hateful to an Egyptian; he became
A shepherd, and led his flocks and herds amid
The solitudes and wilds of Midian, where he
Nursed in silent loneliness his earnest faith
In God and a constant love for kindred, tribe
And race. Years stole o'er him, but they took
No atom from his strength, nor laid one heavy
    weight
Upon his shoulders. The down upon his face
Had ripened to a heavy beard; the fire
That glowed within his youthful eye had deepened
To a calm and steady light, and yet his heart
Was just as faithful to his race as when he had
Stood in Pharaoh's courts and bade farewell
Unto his daughter.
There was a look of patient waiting on his face,
A calm, grand patience, like one who had lifted
Up his eyes to God and seen, with meekened face,
The wings of some great destiny o'ershadowing
All his life with strange and solemn glory.
But the hour came when he must pass from thought
To action,—when the hope of many years

Must reach its grand fruition, and Israel's
Great deliverance dawn. It happened thus:
One day, as Moses led his flocks, he saw
A fertile spot skirted by desert sands,—
A pleasant place for flocks and herds to nip
The tender grass and rest within its shady nooks;
And as he paused and turned, he saw a bush with fire
Aglow; from root to stem a lambent flame
Sent up its jets and sprays of purest light,
And yet the bush, with leaves uncrisped, uncurled,
Was just as green and fresh as if the breath
Of early spring were kissing every leaf.
Then Moses said I'll turn aside to see
This sight, and as he turned he heard a voice
Bidding him lay his sandals by, for Lo! he
Stood on holy ground. Then Moses bowed his head
Upon his staff and spread his mantle o'er
His face, lest he should see the dreadful majesty
Of God; and there, upon that lonely spot,
By Horeb's mount, his shrinking hands received
The burden of his God, which bade him go
To Egypt's guilty king, and bid him let
The oppressed go free.
                         Commissioned thus
He gathered up his flocks and herds and sought
The tents of Jethro, and said " I pray thee
Let me go and see if yet my kindred live;
And Jethro bade him go in peace, nor sought
To throw himself across the purpose of his soul.

Yet there was a tender parting in that home ;
There were moistened eyes, and quivering lips,
And lingering claspings of the parting hand, as Jethro
And his daughters stood within the light of that
Clear morn, and gave to Moses and his wife
And sons their holy wishes and their sad farewells.
For he had been a son and brother in that home
Since first with manly courtesy he had filled
The empty pails of Reuel's daughters, and found
A shelter 'neath his tent when flying from
The wrath of Pharaoh.
              They journeyed on,
Moses, Zipporah and sons, she looking back
With tender love upon the home she had left,
With all its precious memories crowding round
Her heart, and he with eager eyes tracking
His path across the desert, longing once more
To see the long-lost faces of his distant home,
The loving eyes so wont to sun him with their
Welcome, and the aged hands that laid upon
His youthful head their parting blessing. They
Journeyed on till morning's flush and noonday
Splendor glided into the softened, mellowed
Light of eve, and the purple mists were deep'ning
On the cliffs and hills, when Horeb, dual
Crowned, arose before him ; and there he met
His brother Aaron, sent by God to be
His spokesman and to bear him company
To Pharaoh. Tender and joyous was their greeting

They talked of home and friends until the lighter
Ripple of their tnoughts in deeper channels flowed;
And then they talked of Israel's bondage,
And the great deliverance about to dawn
Upon the fortunes of their race; and Moses
Told him of the burning bush, and how the message
Of his God was trembling on his lips.   And thus
They talked until the risen moon had veiled
The mount in soft and silvery light; and then
They rested until morn, and rising up, refreshed
From sleep, pursued their way until they reached
The land of Goshen, and gathered up the elders
Of their race, and told them of the message
Of their Father's God.   Then eager lips caught up
The words of hope and passed the joyful " news
Around, and all the people bowed their heads
And lifted up their hearts in thankfulness
To God."
                              That same day
Moses sought an audience with the king.   He found
Him on his throne surrounded by the princes
Of his court, who bowed in lowly homage
At his feet.   And Pharaoh heard with curving lip
And flushing cheek the message of the Hebrew's God
Then asked in cold and scornful tones, " Has
Israel a God, and if so where has he dwelt
For ages?   As the highest priest of Egypt
I have prayed to Isis, and the Nile has
Overflowed her banks and filled the land

With plenty, but these poor slaves have cried untc
Their God, then crept in want and sorrow
To their graves. Surely Mizraim's God is strong
And Israel's is weak ; then wherefore should
I heed his voice, or at his bidding break
A single yoke ?'' Thus reasoned that proud king,
And turned a deafened ear unto the words
Of Moses and his brother, and yet he felt
Strangely awed before their presence, because
They stood as men who felt the grandeur
Of their mission, and thought not of themselves,
But of their message.

CHAPTER V.

On the next day Pharaoh called a council
Of his mighty men, and before them laid
The message of the brethren : then Amorphel,
Keeper of the palace and nearest lord
Unto the king, arose, and bending low
Before the throne, craved leave to speak a word.
Amorphel was a crafty, treacherous man,
With oily lips well versed in flattery
And courtly speech, a supple reed ready
To bend before his royal master's lightest
Breath—Pharaoh's willing tool.   He said
" Gracious king, thou has been too lenient
With these slaves ; light as their burdens are, they

Fret and chafe beneath them. They are idle
And the blood runs riot in their veins. Now
If thou would'st have these people dwell in peace,
Increase, I pray thee, their tasks and add unto
Their burdens; if they faint beneath their added
Tasks, they will have less time to plot sedition
And revolt."

Then Rhadma, oldest lord in Pharaoh's court,
Arose. He was an aged man, whose white
And heavy beard hung low upon his breast,
Yet there was a hard cold glitter in his eye,
And on his face a proud and evil look.
He had been a servant to the former king,
And wore his signet ring upon his hand.
He said, "I know this Moses well. Fourscore
Years ago Princess Charmian found him
By the Nile and rescued him from death, and did
Choose him as her son, and had him versed in all
The mysteries and lore of Egypt. But blood
Will tell, and this base slave, with servile blood
Within his veins, would rather be a servant
Than a prince, and so, with rude and reckless hand,
He thrust aside the honors of our dear
Departed king. Pharaoh was justly wroth,
But for his daughter's sake he let the trespass
Pass. But one day this Moses slew an Egyptian
In his wrath, and then the king did seek his life;
But he fled, it is said, unto the deserts

Of Arabia, and became a shepherd for the priest
Of Midian. But now, instead of leading flocks
And herds, he aspires to lead his captive race
To freedom. These men mean mischief; sedition
And revolt are in their plans. Decree, I pray thee,
That these men shall gather their own straw
And yet their tale of bricks shall be the same."
And these words pleased Pharaoh well, and all his
Lords chimed in with one accord. And Pharaoh
Wrote the stern decree and sent it unto Goshen—
That the laborers should gather their own straw,
And yet they should not 'minish of their tale of bricks
            'Twas a sad day in Goshen;
The king's degree hung like a gloomy pall
Around their homes. The people fainted 'neath
Their added tasks, then cried unto the king,
That he would ease their burdens; but he hissed
A taunt into their ears and said, " ye are
Idle, and your minds are filled with vain
And foolish thoughts; get you unto your tasks,
And ye shall not 'minish of your tale of bricks."
            And then they turned their eyes
Reproachfully on Moses and his brother,
And laid the cruel blame upon their shoulders.
'Tis an old story now, but then 'twas new
Unto the brethren,—how God's anointed ones
Must walk with bleeding feet the paths that turn
To lines of living light; how hands that bring
Salvation in their palms are pierced with cruel

Nails, and lips that quiver first with some **great truth**
Are steeped in bitterness and tears, and brows
Now bright beneath the aureola of God,
Have bent beneath the thorny crowns of earth.
     There was hope for Israel,
But they did not see the golden fringes
Of their coming morn; they only saw the cold,
Grey sky, and fainted 'neath the cheerless gloom.

Moses sought again the presence of the king:
And Pharaoh's brow grew dark with wrath,
And rising up in angry haste, he said,
Defiantly, "If thy God be great, show
Us some sign or token of his power."
Then Moses threw his rod upon the floor,
And it trembled with a sign of life;
The dark wood glowed, then changed into a thing
Of glistening scales and golden rings, and green,
And brown and purple stripes; a hissing, hateful
Thing, that glared its fiery eye, and darting forth
From Moses' side, lay coiled and panting
At the monarch's feet.   With wonder open-eyed
The king gazed on the changed rod, then called
For his magicians—wily men, well versed
In sinful lore—and bade them do the same.
And they, leagued with the powers of night, did
Also change their rods to serpents; then Moses'
Serpent darted forth, and with a startling hiss
And angry gulp, he swallowed the living things

That coiled along his path.   And thus did Moses
Show that Israel's God had greater power
Than those dark sons of night.

               But not by this alone
Did God his mighty power reveal : He changed
Their waters ; every fountain, well and pool
Was red with blood, and lips, all parched with thirst,
Shrank back in horror from the crimson draughts.
And then the worshiped Nile grew full of life :
Millions of frogs swarmed from the stream—they
    clogged
The pathway of the priests and filled the sacred
Fanes, and crowded into Pharaoh's bed, and hopped
Into his trays of bread, and slumbered in his
Ovens and his pans.

Then came another plague, of loathsome vermin ;
They were gray and creeping things, that made
Their very clothes alive with dark and sombre
Spots—things so loathsome in the land they did
Suspend the service of the temple ; for no priest
Dared to lift his hand to any god with one
Of these upon him.   And then the sky grew
Dark, as if a cloud were passing o'er its
Changeless blue ; a buzzing sound broke o'er
The city, and the land was swarmed with flies.
The murrain laid their cattle low ; the hail
Cut off the first fruits of the Nile ; the locusts,
With their hungry jaws, destroyed the later crops,

And left the ground as brown and bare as if a fire
Had scorched it through,
              Then angry blains
And fiery boils did blur the flesh of man
And beast; and then for three long days, nor saffron
Tint, nor crimson flush, nor soft and silvery light
Divided day from morn, nor told the passage
Of the hours; men rose not from their seats, but sat
In silent awe.　That lengthened night lay like a
    burden
On the air,—a darkness one might almost gather
In his hand, it was so gross and thick.　Then came
The last dread plague—the death of the first born.
              'Twas midnight,
And a startling shriek rose from each palace,
Home and hut of Egypt, save the blood-besprinkled
    homes
Of Goshen; the midnight seemed to shiver with a
    sense
Of dread, as if the mystic angels wing
Had chilled the very air with horror.
Death! Death! was everywhere—in every home
A corpse—in every heart a bitter woe.
There were anxious fingerings for the pulse
That ne'er would throb again, and eager listenings
For some sound of life—a hurrying to and fro—
Then burning kisses on the cold lips
Of the dead, bitter partings, sad farewells,
And mournful sobs and piercing shrieks,

And eep and heavy groans throughout the length
And breadth of Egypt. 'Twas the last dread plague,
But it had snapped in twain the chains on which
The rust of ages lay, and Israel was freed;
Not only freed, but thrust in eager haste
From out the land. Trembling men stood by, and
    longed
To see them gather up their flocks and herds,
And household goods, and leave the land; because
    they felt
That death stood at their doors as long as Israel
Lingered there; and they went forth in haste,
To tread the paths of freedom.

CHAPTER VI.

But Pharaoh was strangely blind, and turning
From his first-born and his dead, with Egypt's wail
Scarce still upon his ear, he asked which way had
Israel gone? They told him that they journeyed
Towards the mighty sea, and were encamped
Near Baalzephn.
Then Pharaoh said, "the wilderness will hem them in,
The mighty sea will roll its barriers in front,
And with my chariots and my warlike men
I'll bring them back, or mete them out their graves."
        Then Pharaoh's officers arose
And gathered up the armies of the king
And made his chariots ready for pursuit.

With proud escutcheons blazoned to the sun,
In his chariot of ivory, pearl and gold,
Pharaoh rolled out of Egypt; and with him
Rode his mighty men, their banners floating
On the breeze, their spears and armor glittering
In the morning light; and Israel saw,
With fainting hearts, their old oppressors on their
Track : then women wept in hopeless terror ;
Children hid their faces in their mothers' robes,
And strong men bowed their heads in agony and
    dread ;
A nd then a bitter, angry murmur rose,—
" Were there no graves in Egypt, that thou hast
B rought us here to die ?"
Then Moses lifted up his face, aglow
With earnest faith in God, and bade their fainting
    hearts
Be strong and they should his salvation see.
" Stand still," said Moses to the fearful throng
Whose hearts were fainting in the wild, " Stand still
Ah, that was Moses' word, but higher and greater
Came God's watchword for the hour, and not for that
 Alone, but all the coming hours of time.
"Speak ye unto the people and bid them
Forward go ; stretch thy hand across the waters
And smite them with thy rod." And Moses smote
The restless sea ; the waves stood up in heaps,
Then lay as calm and still as lips that just
Had tasted death. The secret-loving sea

Laid bare her coral caves and iris-tinted
Floor; that wall of flood which lined the people's
Way was God's own wondrous masonry;
The signal pillar sent to guide them through the wild
Moved its dark shadow till it fronted Egypt's
Camp, but hung in fiery splendor, a light
To Israel's path.   Madly rushed the hosts
Of Pharaoh upon the people's track, when
The solemn truth broke on them—that God
For Israel fought.   With cheeks in terror
Blenching, and eyes astart with fear, " let
Us flee," they cried, " from Israel, for their God
Doth fight against us; he is battling on their side."
They had trusted in their chariots, but now
That hope was vain ; God had loosened every
Axle and unfastened every wheel, and each
Face did gather blackness and each heart stood still
With fear, as the livid lightnings glittered
And the thunder roared and muttered on the air,
And they saw the dreadful ruin that shuddered
O'er their heads, for the waves began to tremble
And the wall of flood to bend.   Then arose
A cry of terror, baffled hate and hopeless dread,
A gurgling sound of horror, as " the waves
Came madly dashing, wildly crashing, seeking
Out their place again," and the flower and pride
Of Egypt sank as lead within the sea
Till the waves threw back their corpses cold and
    stark

Upon the shore, and the song of Israel's
Triumph was the requiem of their foes.
Oh the grandeur of that triumph ; up the cliffs
And down the valleys, o'er the dark and restless
Sea, rose the people's shout of triumph, going
Up in praise to God, and the very air
Seemed joyous for the choral song of millions
Throbbed upon its viewless wings.
Then another song of triumph rose in accents
Soft and clear; " 'twas the voice of Moses' sister
Rising in the tide of song. The warm blood
Of her childhood seemed dancing in her veins ;
The roses of her girlhood were flushing
On her cheek, and her eyes flashed out the splendor
Of long departed days, for time itself seemed
Pausing, and she lived the past again ; again
The Nile flowed by her; she was watching by the
    stream,
A little ark of rushes where her baby brother lay ;
The tender tide of rapture swept o'er her soul again
She had felt when Pharaoh's daughter had claimed
Him as her own, and her mother wept for joy
Above her rescued son. Then again she saw
Him choosing " 'twixt Israel's pain and sorrow
And Egypt's pomp and pride." But now he stood
Their leader triumphant on that shore, and loud
She struck the cymbals as she led the Hebrew women
In music, dance and song, as they shouted out
Triumphs in sweet and glad refrains.

MIRIAM'S SONG.

A wail in the palace, a wail in the hut,
  The midnight is shivering with dread,
And Egypt wakes up with a shriek and a sob
  To mourn for her first-born and dead.

In the morning glad voices greeted the light,
  As the Nile with its splendor was flushed;
At midnight silence had melted their tones,
  And their music forever is hushed.

In the morning the princes of palace and court
  To the heir of the kingdom bowed down;
'Tis midnight, pallid and stark in his shroud
  He dreams not of kingdom or crown.

As a monument blasted and blighted by God,
  Through the ages proud Pharaoh shall stand,
All seamed with the vengeance and scarred with the wrath
  That leaped from God's terrible hand.

CHAPTER VII.

They journeyed on from Zuphim's sea until
They reached the sacred mount and heard the solemn
Decalogue. The mount was robed in blackness,—
Heavy and deep the shadows lay; the thunder
Crashed and roared upon the air; the lightning
Leaped from crag to crag; God's fearful splendor
Flowed around, and Sinai quaked and shuddered
To its base, and there did God proclaim
Unto their listening ears, the great, the grand,

The central and the primal truth of all
The universe—the unity of God.
                    Only one God,—
This truth received into the world's great life,
Not as an idle dream nor speculative thing,
But as a living, vitalizing thought,
Should bind us closer to our God and link us
With our fellow man, the brothers and co-heirs
With Christ, the elder brother of our race.
Before this truth let every blade of war
Grow dull, and slavery, cowering at the light,
Skulk from the homes of men; instead
Of war bring peace and freedom, love and joy,
And light for man, instead of bondage, whips
And chains. Only one God! the strongest hands
Should help the weak who bend before the blasts
Of life, because if God is only one
Then we are the children of his mighty hand,
And when we best serve man, we also serve
Our God. Let haughty rulers learn that men
Of humblest birth and lowliest lot have
Rights as sacred and divine as theirs, and they
Who fence in leagues of earth by bonds and claims
And title deeds, forgetting land and water,
Air and light are God's own gifts and heritage
For man—who throw their selfish lives between
God's sunshine and the shivering poor—
Have never learned the wondrous depth, nor scaled
The glorious height of this great central truth,

Around which clusters all the holiest faiths
Of earth.   The thunder died upon the air,
The lightning ceased its livid play, the smoke
And darkness died away in clouds, as soft
And fair as summer wreaths that lie around
The setting sun, and Sinai stood a bare
And rugged thing among the sacred scenes
Of earth.

Chapter VIII.

It was a weary thing to bear the burden
Of that restless and rebellious race.   With
Sinai's thunders almost crashing in their ears,
They made a golden calf, and in the desert
Spread an idol's feast, and sung the merry songs
They had heard when Mizraim's songs bowed down
  before
Their vain and heathen gods; and thus for many
  years
Did Moses bear the evil manners of his race—
Their angry murmurs, fierce regrets and strange
Forgetfulness of God.   Born slaves, they did not love
The freedom of the wild more than their pots of
  flesh.
And pleasant savory things once gathered
From the gardens of the Nile.
If slavery only laid its weight of chains

Upon the weary, aching limbs, e'en then
It were a curse; but when it frets through nerve
And flesh and eats into the weary soul,
Oh then it is a thing for every human
Heart to loathe, and this was Israel's fate,
For when the chains were shaken from their limits
They failed to strike the impress from their souls.
While he who'd basked beneath the radiance
Of a throne, ne'er turned regretful eyes upon
The past, nor sighed to grasp again the pleasures
Once resigned; but the saddest trial was
To see the light and joy fade from their faces
When the faithless spies spread through their camp
Their ill report; and when the people wept
In hopeless unbelief and turned their faces
Egyptward, and asked a captain from their bands
To lead them back where they might bind anew
Their broken chains, when God arose and shut
The gates of promise on their lives, and left
Their bones to bleach beneath Arabia's desert sands
But though they slumbered in the wild, they died
With broader freedom on their lips, and for their
Little ones did God reserve the heritage
So rudely thrust aside.

THE DEATH OF MOSES.— Chapter IX.

His work was done ; his blessing lay
Like precious ointment on his people's head,
And God's great peace was resting on his soul.
His life had been a lengthened sacrifice,
A thing of deep devotion to his race,
Since first he turned his eyes on Egypt's gild
And glow, and clasped their fortunes in his hand
And held them with a firm and constant grasp.
But now his work was done ; his charge was laid
In Joshua's hand, and men of younger blood
Were destined to possess the land and pass
Through Jordan to the other side.   He too
Had hoped to enter there—to tread the soil
Made sacred by the memories of his
Kindred dead, and rest till life's calm close beneath
The sheltering vines and stately palms of that
Fair land ; that hope had colored all his life's
Young dreams and sent its mellowed flushes o'er
His later years ; but God's decree was otherwise.
And so he bowed his meekened soul in calm
Submission to the word, which bade him climb
To Nebo's highest peak, and view the pleasant land
From Jordan's swells unto the calmer ripples
Of the tideless sea, then die with all its
Loveliness in sight.
As he passed from Moab's grassy vale to climb

The rugged mount, the people stood in mournful
  groups,
Some, with quivering lips and tearful eyes,
Reaching out unconscious hands, as if to stay
His steps and keep him ever at their side, while
Others gazed with reverent awe upon
The calm and solemn beauty on his aged brow,
The look of loving trust and lofty faith
Still beaming from an eye that neither care
Nor time had dimmed. As he passed upward, tender
Blessings, earnest prayers and sad farewells rose
On each wave of air, then died in one sweet
Murmur of regretful love; and Moses stood
Alone on Nebo's mount.

                        Alone! not one
Of all that mighty throng who had trod with him
In triumph through the parted flood was there.
Aaron had died in Hor, with son and brother
By his side; and Miriam too was gone.
But kindred hands had made her grave, and Kadesh
Held her dust. But he was all alone; nor wife
Nor child was there to clasp in death his hand,
And bind around their bleeding hearts the precious
Parting words. And yet he was not all alone,
For God's great presence flowed around his path
And stayed him in that solemn hour.

He stood upon the highest peak of Nebo,
And saw the Jordan chafing through its gorges,

Its banks made bright by scarlet blooms
And purple blossoms.   The placid lakes
And emerald meadows, the snowy crest
Of distant mountains, the ancient rocks
That dripped with honey, the hills all bathed
In light and beauty ; the shady groves
And peaceful vistas, the vines opprest
With purple riches, the fig trees fruit-crowned
Green and golden, the pomegranates with crimson
Blushes, the olives with their darker clusters,
Rose before him like a vision, full of beauty
And delight.   Gazed he on the lovely landscape
Till it faded from his view, and the wing
Of death's sweet angel hovered o'er the mountain's
Crest, and he heard his garments rustle through
The watches of the night.

              Then another, fairer, vision
Broke upon his longing gaze ; 'twas the land
Of crystal fountains, love and beauty, joy
And light, for the pearly gates flew open,
And his ransomed soul went in.   And when morning
O'er the mountain fringed each crag and peak with
    light,
Cold and lifeless lay the leader.   God had touched
His eyes with slumber, giving his beloved sleep.

        Oh never on that mountain
        Was seen a lovelier sight
        Than the troupe of fair young angels
        That gathered 'round the dead.

With gentle hands they bore him
That bright and shining train,
From Nebo's lonely mountain
To sleep in Moab's vale.
But they sung no mornful dirges
No solemn requiems said,
And the soft wave of their pinions
Made music as they trod.
But no one heard them passing,
None saw their chosen grave ;
It was the angels secret
Where Moses should be laid.
And when the grave was finished
They trod with golden sandals
Above the sacred spot,
And the brightest, fairest flower
Sprang up beneath their tread
Nor broken turf, nor hillock
Did e'er reveal that grave,
And truthful lips have never said
We know where he is laid.

THE MISSION OF THE FLOWERS.

In a lovely garden, filled with fair and blooming flowers, stood a beautiful rose tree. It was the centre of attraction, and won the admiration of every eye; its beauteous flowers were sought to adorn the bridal wreath and deck the funeral bier. It was a thing of joy and beauty, and its earth mission was a blessing. Kind hands plucked its flowers to gladden the chamber of sickness and adorn the prisoner's lonely cell. Young girls wore them 'mid their clustering curls, and grave brows relaxed when they gazed upon their wondrous beauty. Now the rose was very kind and generous hearted, and, seeing how much joy she dispensed, wished that every flower could only be a rose, and like herself have the privilege of giving joy to the children of men; and while she thus mused, a bright and lovely spirit approached her and said, "I know thy wishes and will grant thy desires. Thou shalt have power to change every flower in the garden to thine own likeness. When the soft winds come wooing thy fairest buds and flowers, thou shalt breathe gently

of thy sister plants, and beneath thy influence they
small change to beautiful roses." The rose tree
bowed her head in silent gratitude to the gentle being
who had granted her this wondrous power. All nigh·
the stars bent over her from their holy homes above,
but she scarcely heeded their vigils. The gentle dews
nestled in her arms and kissed the cheeks of her
daughters; but she hardly noticed them;—she was
waiting for the soft airs to awaken and seek her
charming abode. At length the gentle airs greeted
her, and she hailed them with a joyous welcome, and
then commenced her work of change. The first object
that met her vision was a tulip superbly arrayed in
scarlet and gold. When she was aware of the intention of her neighbor, her cheeks flamed with anger,
her eyes flashed indignantly, and she haughtily refused
to change her proud robes for the garb the rose tree
had prepared for her; but she could not resist the spell
that was upon her, and she passively permitted the
garments of the rose to enfold her yielding limbs. The
verbenas saw the change that had fallen upon the tulip
and dreading that a similar fate awaited them, crept
closely to the ground, and, while tears gathered in their
eyes, they felt a change pass through their sensitive
frames, and instead of gentle verbenas they were
blushing roses. She breathed upon the sleepy poppies;
a deeper slumber fell upon their senses, and when they
awoke, they too had changed to bright and beautiful
roses. The heliotrope read her fate in the lot of her

sisters, and, bowing her fair head in silent sorrow, gracefully submitted to her unwelcome destiny. The violets, whose mission was to herald the approach of spring, were averse to losing their identity. "Surely," said they, "we have a mission as well as the rose;" but with heavy hearts they saw themselves changed like their sister plants. The snow drop drew around her her robes of virgin white; she would not willingly exchange them for the most brilliant attire that ever decked a flower's form; to her they were the emblems of purity and innocence; but the rose tree breathed upon her, and with a bitter sob she reluctantly consented to the change. The dahlias lifted their heads proudly and defiantly; they dreaded the change, but scorned submission; they loved the fading year, and wished to spread around his dying couch their brightest, fairest flowers; but vainly they struggled, the doom was upon them, and they could not escape. A modest lily that grew near the rose tree shrank instinctively from her; but it was in vain, and with tearful eyes and trembling limbs she yielded, while a quiver of agony convulsed her frame. The marygolds sighed submissively and made no remonstrance. The garden pinks grew careless, and submitted without a murmur, while other flowers, less fragrant or less fair, paled with sorrow or reddened with anger; but the spell of the rose tree was upon them, and every flower was changed by her power, and that once beautiful garden was overran with roses; it had become a perfect wilderness of roses; the garden had changed, but that variety which had lent it so much beauty was gone, and men grew tired of roses, for they were everywhere. The smallest violet peeping faintly from its bed would have been welcome, the humblest primrose would have been hailed with delight,—even a dandelion would have been a harbinger of joy; and when the rose saw that the children of men were dissatisfied with the change she had made, her heart grew sad within her, and she wished the power had never been given her to change her sister plants to roses, and tears came into her eyes as she mused, when suddenly a rough wind shook her drooping form, and she opened her eyes and found that she had only been dreaming. But an important lesson had been taught; she had learned to respect the individuality of her sister flowers, and began to see that they, as well as herself, had their own missions, —some to gladden the eye with their loveliness and thrill the soul with delight; some to transmit fragrance to the air; others to breathe a refining influence upon the world; some had power to lull the aching brow and soothe the weary heart and brain into forgetfulness; and of those whose mission she did not understand, she wisely concluded there must be some object in their creation, and resolved to be true to her own earth-mission, and lay her fairest buds and flowers upon the altars of love and truth.

THE RAGGED STOCKING.

Do you see this ragged stocking,
   Here a rent and there a hole?
Each thread of this little stocking
   Is woven around my soul.

Do you wish to hear my story?
   Excuse me, the tears will start,
For the sight of this ragged stocking
   Stirs the fountains of my heart.

You say that my home is happy;
   To me 'tis earth's fairest place,
But its sunshine, peace and gladness
   Back to this stocking I trace.

I was once a wretched drunkard;
   Ah! you start and say not so;
But the dreadful depths I've sounded,
   And I speak of what I know.

I was wild and very reckless
   When I stood on manhood's brink,
And, joining with pleasure-seekers
   Learned to revel and drink.

Strong drink is a raging demon,
   In his hands are shame and woe;
He mocketh the strength of the mighty
   And bringeth the strong man low.

The light of my home was darkened
  By the shadow of my sin;
And want and woe unbarr'd the **door,**
  And suffering entered in.

*   *   *   *   *   *   *   *

The streets were full one Christmas eve,
  And alive with girls and boys,
Merrily looking through window-panes
  At bright and beautiful toys.

And throngs of parents came to **buy**
  The gifts that children prize,
And homeward trudged with happy **hearts,**
  The love-light in their eyes.

I thought of my little Charley
  At home in his lowly bed,
With the shadows around his life,
  And in shame I bowed my **head.**

I entered my home a sober man,
  My heart by remorse was wrung,
And there in the chimney corner,
  This little stocking was hung.

Faded and worn as you see it;
  To me 'tis a precious thing,
And I never gaze upon it
  But unbidden tears will spring.

  4

I began to search my pockets,
　　But scarcely a dime was there;
But scanty as was the pittance,
　　This stocking received its share.

For a longing seized upon me
　　To gladden the heart of my boy,
And I bought him some cakes and candy,
　　And added a simple toy.

Then I knelt by this little stocking
　　And sobbed out an earnest prayer,
And arose with strength to wrestle
　　And break from the tempter's snare.

And this faded, worn-out stocking,
　　So pitiful once to see,
Became the wedge that broke my chain,
　　And a blessing brought to me.

Do you marvel then I prize it?
　　When each darn and seam and hole
Is linked with my soul's deliverance
　　From the bondage of the bowl?

And to night my wife will tell you,
　　Though I've houses, gold and land,
He holds no treasure more precious
　　Than this stocking in my hand.

THE FATAL PLEDGE.

"Pledge me with wine," the maiden cried,
  Her tones were gay and light;
"From others you have turned aside,
  I claim your pledge to-night."

The blood rushed to the young man's cheek
  Then left it deadly pale;
Beneath the witchery of her smile
  He felt his courage fail.

For many years he'd been a slave
  To the enchanting bowl,
Until he grasped with eager hands
  The reins of self-control;

And struggled with his hated thrall,
  Until he rent his chain,
And strove to stand erect and free,
  And be a man again.

When others came with tempting words
  He coldly turned aside,
But she who held the sparkling cup
  Was his affianced bride;

And like a vision of delight,
  Bright, beautiful and fair,
With thoughtless words she wove for him
  The meshes of despair.

From jeweled hands he took the cup,
   Nor heard the serpent's hiss;
Nor saw beneath its ruby glow
   The deadly adder's hiss.

Like waves that madly, wildly dash,
   When dykes are overthrown,
The barriers of his soul gave way,
   Each life with wrecks was strewn.

And she who might have reached her hand
   To succor and to save,
Soon wept in hopeless agony
   Above a drunkard's grave.

And bore through life with bleeding heart
   Remembrance of that night,
When she had urged the tempted man
   With wine to make his plight.

CHRIST'S ENTRY INTO JERUSALEM.

He had plunged into our sorrows,
   And our sin had pierced his heart,
As before him loomed death's shadow,
   And he knew he must depart.

But they hailed him as a victor
   As he into Salem came,
And the very children shouted
   Loud hosannas to his name.

But he knew behind that triumph,
   Rising gladly to the sky,
Soon would come the cries of malice:
   Crucify him! Crucify!

Onward rode the blessed Saviour,
   Conscious of the coming strife
Soon to break in storms of hatred
   Round his dear, devoted life.

Ghastly in its fearful anguish
   Rose the cross before his eyes,
But he saw the joy beyond it,
   And did all the shame despise.

Joy to see the cry of scorning
   Through the ages ever bright,
And the cross of shame transfigured
   To a throne of love and light.

Joy to know his soul's deep travail
  Should not be a thing in vain,
And that joy and peace should blossom
  From his agonizing pain.

———

THE RESURRECTION OF JESUS.

It was done, the deed of horror;
  Christ had died upon the cross,
And within an upper chamber
  The disciples mourned their loss.

Peter's eyes were full of anguish,
  Thinking sadly of the trial
When his boasted self-reliance
  Ended in his Lord's denial.

Disappointment, deep and heavy,
  Shrouded every heart with gloom,
As the hopes so fondly cherished
  Died around the garden tomb.

And they thought with shame and sorrow
  How they fled in that dark hour,
When they saw their Lord and Master
  In the clutch of Roman power.

We had hoped, they sadly uttered,
  He would over Israel reign,
But to-day he lies sepulchred,
  And our cherished hopes are vain.

In the humble home of Mary
   Slowly waned the hours away,
Till she rose to seek the garden
   And the place where Jesus lay.

Not the cross with all its anguish
   Could her loving heart restrain,
But the tomb she sought was empty,
   And her heart o'erflowed with pain.

To embalm my Lord and Master
   To this garden I have strayed,
But, behold, I miss his body,
   And I know not where he's laid.

Then a wave of strange emotion
   Swept her soul, as angels said,
" Wherefore do ye seek the living
   'Mid the chambers of the dead? "

Unperceived, her Lord stood by her,
   Silent witness of her grief,
Bearing on his lips the tidings
   Sure to bring a glad relief.

But her tear-dimmed eyes were holden
   When she heard the Master speak ;
Thought she, only 'tis the gardener
   Asking whom her soul did seek.

Then a sudden flush of gladness
  O'er her grief-worn features spread;
When she knew the voice of Jesus
  All her bitter anguish fled.

Forth she reached hands in rapture.
  Touch me not, the Saviour said;
Take the message to my brethren,
  I have risen from the dead.

Take them words of joy and comfort,
  Which will all their mourning end;
To their Father and my Father,
  Tell them that I will ascend.

"Brethren, I have seen the Master:
  He is risen from the dead."
But like words of idle meaning
  Seemed the glorious words she said.

Soon they saw the revelation
  Which would bid their mourning cease:
Christ, the risen, stood before them
  Breathing words of love and peace.

Timid men were changed to heroes,
  Weakness turned to wondrous might,
And the cross became their standard,
  Luminous with love and light.

From that lonely upper chamber,
  Holding up the rugged cross,
With a glad and bold surrender
  They encountered shame and loss.

In these days of doubt and error,
  In the conflict for the right,
May our hearts be ever strengthened
  By the resurrection's might.

———

SIMON'S COUNTRYMEN.

They took away his seamless robe,
  With thorns they crowned his head,
As harshly, fiercely cried his foes:
  "Barabbas in his stead."

The friends he loved unto the end,
  Who shared his daily bread,
Before the storms of wrath and hate
  Forsook their Lord and fled.

To rescue men from death and sin
  He knew the awful cost,
As wearily he bent beneath
  The burden of the cross.

When Pilate had decreed his fate,
  And Jews withheld their aid,
Then Simon, the Cyrenean, came:
  On him the cross was laid.

Not his to smite with cruel scorn,
   Nor mock the dying one,
That helpful man came from the land
   Kissed by the ardent sun—

The land within whose sheltering arms
   The infant Jesus lay
When Herod vainly bared his sword
   And sought the child to slay.

Amid the calendar of saints
   We Simon's name may trace,
On history's page thro' every age
   He bears an honored place.

He little knew that cross would change
   Unto a throne of light;
The crown of thorns upon Christ's brow
   Would be forever bright.

Beneath the shadow of that cross
   Brave men with outstretched hands
Have told the wondrous tale of love
   In distant heathen lands.

And yet within our favored land,
   Where Christian churches rise,
The dark-browed sons of Africa
   Are hated and despised.

Can they who speak of Christ as King,
   And glory in his name,

Forget that Simon's countrymen
   Still bear a cross of shame?

Can they forget the cruel scorn
   Men shower on a race
Who treat the hues their Father gives
   As emblems of disgrace?

Will they erect to God their fanes
   And Christ with honor crown,
And then with cruel weights of pain
   The African press down?

Oh, Christians, when we faint and bleed
   In this our native land,
Reach out to us when peeled, opprest,
   A kindly helping hand,

And bear aloft that sacred cross,
   Bright from the distant years,
And say for Christ's and Simon's sake,
   We'll wipe away your tears.

For years of sorrow, toil and pain
   We'll bring you love and light,
And in the name of Christ our Lord
   We'll make your pathway bright.

That seamless robe shall yet enfold
   The children of the sun,
Till rich and poor and bond and free
   In Christ shall all be one.

And for his sake from pride and scorn
  Our spirits shall be free,
Till through our souls shall sound the words
  He did it unto me.

DELIVERANCE.

Rise up! rise up! Oh Israel,
  Let a spotless lamb be slain;
The angel of death will o'er you bend
  And rend your galling chain.

Sprinkle its blood upon the posts
  And lintels of your door;
When the angel sees the crimson spots
  Unharmed he will pass you o'er.

Gather your flocks and herds to-night,
  Your children by your side:
A leader from Arabia comes
  To be your friend and guide.

With girded loins and sandled feet
  Await the hour of dread,
When Mizraim shall wildly mourn
  Her first-born and her dead.

The sons of Abraham no more
  Shall crouch 'neath Pharoah's hand,
Trembling with agony and dread,
  He'll thrust you from the land.

And ye shall hold in unborn years
   A feast to mark this day,
When joyfully the fathers rose
   And cast their chains away.

When crimson tints of morning flush
   The golden gates of day,
Or gorgeous hue of even melt
   In sombre shades away,

Then ye shall to your children teach
   The meaning of this feast,
How from the proud oppressor's hand
   Their fathers were released,

And ye shall hold through distant years
   This feast with glad accord,
And children's children yet shall learn
   To love and trust the Lord.

Ages have passed since Israel trod
   In triumph through the sea,
And yet they hold in memory's urn
   Their first great jubilee.

When Moses led the ransomed hosts,
   And Miriam's song arose,
While ruin closed around the path
   Of their pursuing foes.

Shall Israel thro' long varied years
   These memories cherish yet,
And we who lately stood redeemed
   Our broken chains forget?

Should we forget the wondrous change
   That to our people came,
When justice rose and sternly plead
   Our cause with sword and flame?

And led us through the storms of war
   To freedom's fairer shore,
When slavery sank beneath a flood
   Whose waves were human gore.

Oh, youth and maidens of the land,
   Rise up with one accord,
And in the name of Christ go forth
   To battle for the Lord.

Go forth, but not in crimson fields,
   With fratricidal strife,
But in the name of Christ go forth
   For freedom, love and life.

Go forth to follow in his steps,
   Who came not to destroy,
Till wastes shall blossom as the rose,
   And deserts sing for joy.

SIMON'S FEAST.

He is coming, she said, to Simon's feast,
　The prophet of Galilee,
Though multitudes around him throng
　In longing his face to see.

He enters the home as Simon's guest,
　But he gives no welcome kiss;
He brings no water to bathe his feet—
　Why is Simon so remiss?

The prophet's face is bright with love,
　And mercy beams from his eye;
He pities the poor, the lame and blind,
　An outcast, I will draw nigh.

If a prophet, he will surely know
　The guilt of my darkened years;
With broken heart I'll seek his face,
　And bathe his feet with my tears.

No holy rabbi lays his hand
　In blessing on my head;
No loving voice floats o'er the path,
　The downward path I tread.

Unto the Master's side she pressed,
　A penitent, frail and fair,
Rained on his feet a flood of tears,
　And then wiped them with her hair.

Over the face of Simon swept
  An air of puzzled surprise;
Can my guest a holy prophet be,
  And not this woman despise?

Christ saw the thoughts that Simon's heart
  Had written upon his face,
Kindly turned to the sinful one
  In her sorrow and disgrace.

Where Simon only saw the stains,
  Where sin and shame were rife,
Christ looked beneath and saw the germs
  Of a fair, outflowering life.

Like one who breaks a galling chain,
  And sets a prisoner free,
He rent her fetters with the words,
  "Thy sins are forgiven thee."

God be praised for the gracious words
  Which came through that woman's touch
That souls redeemed thro' God's dear Son
  May learn to love him so much;

That souls once red with guilt and crime
  May their crimson stains outgrow;
The scarlet spots upon their lives
  Become whiter than driven snow.

CONTENTS

ELE

&

ıLSH

HUETZ

PARKER

ıA STERBAK

.NAH VILLIGER

HERMIONE WILTSHIRE

ACKNOWLEDGEMENTS

Tate Gallery Liverpool wishes to thank the following for their help in the preparation of the exhibition:

René Blouin and Anne Delaney,
Galerie René Blouin, Montreal
Canadian High Commission
Pierre Chevalier, Galerie du Jour, Paris
Chantal Crousel, Francine Tagliaferro
and Tracy Williams, Galerie
Crousel-Robelin, Paris
Richard Gagnier, National Gallery of
Canada, Ottawa
Government of Canada
Evelyne Lohm, Kunsthaus Zug
Kate Mellor, British Film Institute
Barry Prothero, Angel Row Gallery,
Nottingham
Galerie Nikolaus Sonne, Berlin
Jonas Storsve, Musée des Beaux-Arts de
Nantes

ISBN 1-85437-126-6
Published by order of the Trustees 1993
for the exhibition
ELECTIVE AFFINITIES
8 September - 7 November 1993
Copyright © 1993 The Tate Gallery
and authors
All rights reserved

Catalogue compiled and edited by
Penelope Curtis
with the assistance of
Jemima Pyne and Helen Ruscoe
at Tate Gallery Liverpool, Albert Dock,
Liverpool L3 4BB

Designed by Jeremy Greenwood,
Woodbridge
Printed by Balding + Mansell, Wisbech

Distributed by
Tate Gallery Publications,
Millbank, London SW1P 4RG

Photographic credits

Angel Row Gallery, Nottingham p 51
British Library p 69
Galerie Crousel-Robelin pp 9, 42
National Gallery of Canada pp 44, 45
Courtesy Galerie René Blouin p 9
Walter Phillips Gallery, Banff p 10
Edward Woodman pp 48, 49, 50, 51,
54, 55, 56, 57

cover
HANNAH VILLIGER
Sculptural 1984-85

In addition to making exhibitions devoted to the work of a single artist, Tate Gallery Liverpool has presented a series of group exhibitions in which a number of artists are introduced to a wider public. Until now the theme underlying such exhibitions has tended to be geographical, and we have made exhibitions of artists from Cologne, the North of Britain, Ireland, Japan, and Korea. The present exhibition has no such basis, given that the artists represented work in Britain, Ireland, Germany, France and Canada. What brings them together is an act of selection which proposes that their work stimulates comparisons.

Elective Affinities has been selected by Penelope Curtis to focus on the connections between the viewer's physical and mental identification with the forms and subjects of recent art. It takes its title from Goethe's novel about inevitable attraction, and similarly sets up the question as to what extent we are free of our own physical impulses.

We are most grateful to all the artists for their commitment to the exhibition, and must thank them both for making new work and for making previous work available. We are also indebted to other lenders - Eric Hattan and Silvia Bäckli, the Kunsthaus Zug, Galerie Crousel-Robelin, Paris, the Musée des Beaux-Arts de Nantes, the National Gallery of Canada and a private collection - who have made it possible to include earlier work in the selection. Penelope Curtis invited Brian Grosskurth of York University, Toronto, and Daria Santini of Rome University to contribute to this catalogue in the belief that they would be able to set up helpful and stimulating juxtapositions between the work on show and the writers Georges Bataille and Goethe. In this they have been extremely successful.

Since the Gallery opened in 1988 it has offered an annual six-month Fellowship supported by the art handling company, Momart. At the end of each of their residencies, the artists, have, in a variety of ways, been involved in presenting their work within the context of the Gallery's wider exhibition programme. We were pleased that Hermione Wiltshire took up our invitation to present her work as part of this group exhibition, and we are indebted to her for the time she gave to discussing the project with Penelope Curtis. Her involvement has contributed significantly to the exhibition.

Nicholas Serota
Director, Tate Gallery

Lewis Biggs
Curator, Tate Gallery Liverpool

INTRODUCTION

Penelope Curtis

The starting point for this exhibition was to find art which involved the spectator - any spectator - immediately, and which makes the body the bridge between the art and the spectator. Fundamental to this art is the fact that its viewers stand in front of it, and physical experience is highlighted or becomes part of its conceptual framework. Whether we like it or not, this work will begin by eliciting a reaction from us which is based on physical recognition.

By establishing (or even exploiting) this initial connection, the work can move on to negotiate more intricate questions. The physical engenders the psychological or philosophical. Much of the meaning in our world relates either actually or metaphorically to the body. The fact that this work evokes a physical affinity also sets up a complicity; the viewer is implicated in the work. In pieces that set up a network of psychological allusion the nature of our involvement is crucial, and it is at this point - as we begin to select our meanings - that we have to begin to exercise personal choice.

In recent British exhibitions the subject of the body has most frequently been related to the question of subject and object; who is looking and who is looked at. They have suggested that the viewer's relationship to the art can depend on their gender. Some of the artists in this exhibition have been involved in forcing just such a recognition, but the selection here is instead about identification, rather than alienation or distanced appraisal. The pieces on show invite some kind of integration of the viewer's presence with the presence of the work. The possibility of identification is frequently assured by the works' liveliness. They use the material itself - photography, film, plaster, glass, bronze - to represent an inner life. Many exploit an elementary identification with material to return us to a more primal level of physical being.

While some works in the exhibition represent the unmediated, undifferentiated body, others represent its meanings by their choice of parts and materials. Though all the works have some things in common with some of the others, there are as many factors of difference. Collectively however they focus their choices, and our readings, on whether to represent the body in part or in whole, open or closed, close-up or distanced, in material or in image, dead or alive. They all use empathy as a way of reading. Analyses of how pornography functions in art provide a useful comparative terminology. Pornography is a language of repetition, convulsion and fragmentation, whose single-mindedness can lead to the loss of self. It is arguable as to whether it works for or against a sense of distance. The work on show here asks us to consider whether or not in the end we do identify the body with the self.

Hannah Villiger

Hannah Villiger photographs her own body with a Polaroid camera which she holds in her hand. This basic procedure means that the representation of the body is inscribed within its own space, within the hand's reach. This sense of a cube - or of a cage - around the body is reinforced by the square format of the Polaroids which are brought up to a uniform dimension of 125 by 123 centimetres, the size envisaged by Villiger as she makes them. There is thus a

strict regularity to the presentation of her work, and space is always the same size. This sense of space - of a certain distance - is crucial to the meaning.

However, despite the importance of distance, Villiger's body is never, and can never be, represented whole. As the camera frames, it fragments. Moreover, Villiger concentrates on certain sections. While some of her work brings us up close without anxiety, others focus on the manipulating of limbs as they appear to strain to fit themselves into the frame. The sense of the body's compression, even contortion, can suggest its imprisonment. The poor quality of the Polaroid photo, and the density of its composition, seem to echo the quality of skin. It has a kind of soft, blemished surface which gives the work a fragility, a kind of dead-alive sensation. The ambiguity of this tenderness is unsettling.

Hannah Villiger was trained in sculpture, in the period when Minimalism was dominant, and she continues to see herself as a sculptor. Her 'Block' works echo the circumnavigation involved in understanding sculpture. She reduces the materiality of sculpture while increasing its hold on our own experience of what it feels like to inhabit a body in space. A knowledge of her education as a sculptor may help us to place the strong three-dimensionality of her work, which exerts a strong pull on its viewers. Some images echo natural gravity; we can identify with the subject almost as we might with choreography. Those images that insist on movement have a gaiety that is not found in the motionless ones. Other pieces subvert vertical gravity, and pull us onto the wall. By using mirrors Villiger opens up the space, helping us to appreciate its underside or interior, but mirrors may also confuse, for they give her limbs their doubles.

Much of Villiger's time is devoted to the arrangement of the single photos into blocks of six or nine, searching for the right amalgam and rhythm of imagery. These blocks can be almost overpowering in their frontality, especially when they combine something that we know is us with elements that are less clear. We are left to wonder not only which part of the body we are seeing, but also what is happening to it. The imagery is at once tender and intrusive; we don't like to be the voyeur.

Though she uses her own body as her subject, there is no sense of revelation about Villiger's work. Rather there is often a sense of hiding, even of cowering, which increases the hint of fear that is run by the viewer. Her works invite the viewer to look, set up an act of engagement, but refuse to bestow a direct answer. Though their light is often harsh, and we might read a relentless interrogation and wounding into some of the pieces, in the end this interrogation seems as much internal as external, for the body is examining itself.

Thomas Florschuetz

Thomas Florschuetz also photographs his own body, though his focus is often much closer, and might suggest a more detailed examination. And though he does not use a Polaroid camera, like Villiger he makes his studies on a small scale, working out his compositions with single frames from the contact sheets of his developed films. Most of his work is carried out at this stage; the actual photographing is often distant in time. He appreciates the forgetting involved in this time lapse, and the fact that the material seems gradually to take on its own order. Thus his work comes down to organizing matter, rather than recreating a specific physical memory.

The notion of matter relates to the body - the body is material, as the photos are material - and by using the body as his motif Florschuetz can evoke the sense of familiarity, the *déja-vu* which particularly interests him. The nexus in his work between matter and meaning is very close to the surface. The intimacy of the close-up borders on wounding, and brings us close to pornography, which operates through the formal fragmentation of the body. But in his photographs Florschuetz provides his selected parts with new bodies, with their own space and gravity. Body parts at once dematerialize and re-acquire weight, hanging like sacks or like curtains. He achieves this materiality - a new wholeness - by asserting the completeness of the image. He weds the part to its background by manipulating symmetry and line, lighting and colour.

Florschuetz's earlier photographs used complex, often multiple, compositions to convey the various aspects of their meaning. His first works, in black and white, carried a narrative which was played out across several consecutive images. They make us think of

THOMAS FLORSCHUETZ
Curtain, 2 Pieces 1993

cinema and the violence of arrested movement, and cinema was an important inspiration for Florschuetz in East Germany. He was interested in how it could tell one story from different viewpoints, and relates this approach to sculpture. He went on to make views of the body which incorporated inset details, providing almost classic demonstrations of the body viewed from close and from far. In other pieces movement was slowed down to a succession of still, almost hierarchical images which hit out silently from single coloured backgrounds.

The new work on show here sheds that element of rhetoric and re-introduces a real sense of movement. Skin – and its softness and transparency – is becoming ever more-important. While earlier works have juxtaposed man's tools with his hands, contrasting the contained and the container, hard and soft, now these implements act more like pointers, revealing the bone beneath the skin, pressing against the body's mortality. The new work reveals Florschuetz's concern to concentrate more in less, bringing together just as large a range of associations but in only one image. A sense of unease is never far away from this range of associations, reminding us of the dark underside of beauty. Florschuetz regards beauty as fragile, and invokes a Baudelairean reading. He works to seduce the viewer, and then to disrupt them. Much of this disruption is carried out on the work's margins, and relies on the inevitable savagery of the camera's frame and on the artist's centering of the edge and the axes. Symmetry and order are almost like an inevitable point of return for him, and one which he fights against. The ruptures within the work thus derive from both internal and external pressures.

Jayne Parker
Jayne Parker's recent films are like poems, with rhyming images which carry themselves in the memory long after their order may have been forgotten. The imagery is both verbal and graphic – a quality intensified by the film being in black and white. Parker puns with images, setting up deliberate *doubles entendres*. The films are put together as if in verses. Like the imagery of poets also, there are certain motifs which recur across more than one film. The over-riding impression of her work is one of great restraint and economy, an economy which allows some of her

chosen material to shed its shocking nature and to take a place within the film in the light of its narrative function. The films' measured choreography exerts its symbolism by allowing the viewer to physically empathise. Perhaps most significantly, their restraint is put to use to convey the process of deliberation. Thought is actively felt by the viewer, the weight of translating thought into action becomes almost painful.

Although Parker has previously chosen to direct others in her films, the trio of films shown here feature the artist herself. The three are closely related, and use the body as a metaphor for experience; for what we have taken in, voluntarily or involuntarily. Their common axis is played around interior/exterior, which brings with it, and is carried through by, further dualities of wet and dry, weight and lightness, falling and lifting, fullness and emptiness, thought and action. One senses that in her films Parker is also an observer; observing how she looks doing something that she finds distasteful. However often she goes through with

JAYNE PARKER
Inside Out 1990

it, one still feels that it has not really impinged. The mind may master the body in these films; but to what extent does the body want to learn?

In the film 'K' Parker expels innards from her body,

8

and is then in a position to knit this matter into a dress with which she shields her own nakedness. Standing on the edge of a swimming pool, she has to repeatedly overcome her fear of falling, her fear of water, as she dives into the pool. We don't see the full sequence - only her hesitation, followed by each exit from the pool - until the last dive.

In 'The Pool' we see black liquid, which we learn to be blood, dripping onto the bottom of a drained pool. The protagonist wipes it off her body routinely but inadequately. The woman who is lifted by the male dancer echoes the lifeless eel which lies balanced across the woman's arms. The eel has previously been seen swimming, breathing through its gills. Breathing out under water the swimmer seems to experience a sense of release.

'Cold Jazz' opens on oyster beds. The protagonist prepares the table; drawing her knife from out of the drawer under the starched linen table-cloth. She forces herself first to prise open and then to eat the oysters. The possible mingling of pain and pleasure, of endurance and foreknowledge, are echoed as she lies by the sea. Do the incoming lapping waves invade or pleasure? Do they give her life as the breath gives life to the saxophone? But the saxophone is invaded in turn, by the cloth which is pulled through its body to dry it. The music seems to give support to the protagonist; though ambiguous, it clearly offsets the possible savagery of the action. The tune is titled 'I can't get started'. This most recent film has a more driven quality about it; the pensiveness of 'The Pool' has given way to something more automatic.

Jana Sterbak

Despite the extremely varied appearance of Sterbak's work over the last fifteen years, a common concern has been to wed the physical to the psychological; placing mind on an equal footing with matter. Many of her

JANA STERBAK
Sisyphus II (detail) 1991

pieces use the human body to carry the desires and constraints of society, and have involved fitting the body into some kind of outer garment. These works question the working of the will, suggesting that we may be freer than we want to be.

The works chosen for this exhibition are among the earliest in Sterbak's oeuvre, and prefigure the more recent trend to fragment the body into its constituent parts. These two pieces bring out the artist's dual concern with the body and with the meaning of materials at their most fundamental levels. They take their place here through their call on an empathetic response from the viewer, and they pin-point that dead-alive quality which is central to art and which this selection seeks to highlight.

The notion of empathy, or 'thinking-in', plays an important role in Sterbak's work. Her installation 'Golem: Objects as Sensations' (1979-82) works on a number of levels, on at least one of which we can all

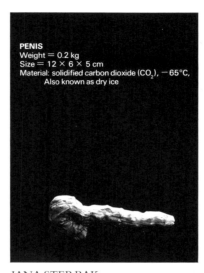
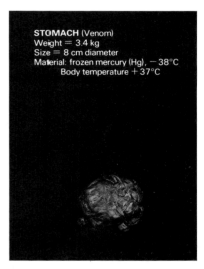

JANA STERBAK
Two silver gelatin prints from *Golem: Objects as Sensations* 1979-82

enter. It comprises three framed prints and parts of the body cast in bronze and lead. The parts are laid out on the ground, like a spine, or a fuse, waiting to come alive. They might make us think of funerary offerings, of votive pieces which represent the function of the organ in life or carry the deceased into afterlife, or of the Roman custom of reading the entrails. More immediately, Sterbak was familiar with the phenomenon of phantom limbs, in which amputees continue to feel sensations connected to their missing limb.

'Golem's' representations of the body's parts - inner and outer - refer us to what the body represents. Each organ - heart, spleen, stomach - has its own significance, and is associated with a humour and with a disease, with both life and death. The outer parts which are included - a hand, a tongue, a penis, an ear, a throat - relate to our body's interaction with the outside world. These parts were first modelled in plasticine, and it was only as Sterbak transposed them into metal, first lead, then bronze, that she became attuned to the seriousness of material. These materials have their own meanings too; their own density and gravity. We are thus brought to a literal consideration of the meaning of materials, not just of what the entrails tell us, but also of what the metals mean. Furthermore, the three photographs purport to re-present a penis in dry-ice, a stomach in frozen mercury, and a heart in radioactive fermium. These portraits of materials take us beyond the object itself into the atmosphere.

Having made 'Golem' Sterbak decided to find out more about physics so as to give further consideration to the specific content of materials, and looked at the Periodic Table. Although Minimalism had been all about understanding material, Sterbak realised that there were many materials - with more exciting properties - which had hardly been explored. The three photographs led her in particular to consider the representation of invisible forces - magnetism, gravity - in art and in science. Physicists since Einstein have been searching for a Unifying Theory which could explain the relationship between gravity, magnetism, electrical, electro-weak and electro-strong forces. This was the relationship which Stephen Hawking was to attempt to explain in his *Short History of Time*.

In 1984 Sterbak made 'I can hear you think (Dedicated to Stephen Hawking)'. Here two solid iron heads lie on the floor; one is isolated, inert, while the other, with its forehead bound with wire, is literally connected to an exterior source of power. By connecting metal wire, a magnetic field and electricity, Sterbak transfers the currents into the head and leaves it alone to experience the reversibility of these forces. This head is literally charged, but we can only imagine its sensations. The use of electricity in this sculpture mirrors the real electrical pulse that signals our own thoughts, and also refers to the associated dangers of harnessing the power of thought. As in other of Sterbak's works the life-giving spark is itself the risk, and consummation can lead to destruction. The idea that the life of the mind is life-giving, or inspirational, may also mean, however, that we will make things in our own form. The divine spark adopts the paternal function of language.

The divine spark that is called to life in 'I can hear you think' refers us back to 'Golem'. The golem is part of Jewish folklore (it means unformed in Hebrew), and the most famous is the Golem of Prague. Making a golem was a stage in Kabbalistic magic, and one of the alchemists' ambitions. A golem is an artificial man, made from the earth, and brought to life with the three other elements; fire, water and breath. This story can be compared to the Greek myth of Prometheus, who made man out of clay, and stole fire for them from Zeus, or to Pygmalion, who falls in love with his own sculpture, whom Athene breathes into life. More recently we have Mary Shelley's *Frankenstein, or the Modern Prometheus* who learns how to give life to inanimate matter. Thus Promethean fire came to be used to describe the divine spark of inspiration. The creation myth is thus intimately linked with destruction.

Helen Chadwick

Helen Chadwick's twelve 'Piss Flowers' shine like snow and froth like fountains. They seem both frozen and moving. Thrusting upwards with their super-stamens, these flowers have a sexual life all of their own. We recognize them as flowers, but they also have something extra-terrestrial about them. The way they sparkle in their stillness, holding their positions across the floor with absolute assurance, gives them the impression of some alien force.

This frozen garden was indeed made in the snows, in the mountains of Northern Canada. Its creation goes back to the winter of 1991, when Chadwick spent four weeks at the Banff Centre for the Arts in Alberta. She had been invited to be an artist-in-residence at the Centre and as an outsider she wanted to make sense of going out into a snowy landscape to make art. Her strategy was to find a way of linking her body with this environment, a line of thinking which is anyway inherent to much of her work.

Chadwick prepared a project in which she and her partner would systematically urinate in the snow to

Helen Chadwick and David Notarius urine casting in Banff National Park, Canada, 1991

create a series of territorial markings. The resulting pattern of melted holes was then to be filled with liquid plaster. The casts would be inverted, so that underground was overground, with the negative becoming positive. Chadwick devised a template which would define the limits of each cast, choosing a five-petalled flower shape which would both contain and give an identifying form to the snow drawings. She urinated first, providing the flower with its central stamen, and her partner then attempted to fill in the surrounding area.

What was at first an elemental but transitory record of human passage - and what seemed like an artistic prank - has become something else, with a beauty all of its own. Moreover the extent to which the 'Piss Flowers' are consistent with Chadwick's major concerns is worth stating. In working directly with her body, Chadwick has allowed an unmediated physical activity to take over from the hand. Thus she places the body on a par with the mind. Her interest in achieving a new balance in the making is part of the meaning of her work. It is one of Chadwick's aims to synthesize contradictory elements, and as the physical is normally contrasted with and designated subservient to the mental, so the female is normally contrasted with the male. In 'Piss Flowers' we have a kind of reconciliation which nevertheless resists our attempts to fix definitions. Their playfulness is that they are continually elusive. Male marks shift into female marks and back again.

Indeed the 'Piss Flowers' seem to encapsulate much of what Chadwick has previously spoken. Recognising that subjectivity is insurmountable - that it is the way in which we interact with the world - much of her work has been about making this realisation concrete. The 'Piss Flowers' are just such an exploration of the point where the body meets the exterior. In Banff they were shown as works in progress with the 'Viral Landscapes', five panoramic photographic prints which Chadwick made in 1989, and which were shown that year at Tate Gallery Liverpool. Chadwick defines all her work as 'constructions in space', and these two works are at once installations, and concrete realisations of the artist's body melting into the world outside. These 'corporeal geographies' - as she describes them - suggest a permeability of boundaries. Knowing that Chadwick has spoken of her wish to 'reunite mind and body as "consciousness" which resides in the relationship between energy and matter' brings us to these casts which combine the rational with animal or sexual instincts, and heat with snow. They give concrete form to a flow that normally has no form, only force.

The original plaster casts for the 'Piss Flowers' looked earthy and ancient, like fossils and stalacmites. Having been cast in bronze and lacquered in white cellulose enamel, they now look very different. No longer completely natural, they have acquired an ethereal life of their own. Though the base and template of the sculptures reveal Chadwick's tendency to order, the upper portion is unusually wild. If we pause to consider, we realise that it is the erect central stamen which embodies the female, and the skirt of froth the male. This is the reverse of what we expect from the flower, and from our analogies between the flower and the human anatomy, and so we have to understand these flowers as hermaphroditic - male and female in origin - like flowers which are self-pollinating. They embrace a dual sexuality and propose a continual cross-referencing in which we see through one gender to the other.

Hermione Wiltshire

Much of Hermione Wiltshire's work has dealt with the relationship between the gender of imagery and the gender of its spectator. Earlier work used the connections between subject and style, or content and art-language, to raise the question of the viewer's expectation. By re-making pornographic imagery in different materials or contexts Wiltshire was effectively able to re-align it. Her concern was to force an acknowledgement that gender comes into our readings of the visual world; an acknowledgement of difference. This developed into a process of making space for her own imagination within her work, rather than concentrating on sources and their readers. Thus where her earlier work used the conventional languages of distancing - both ideologically and actually - her new work, which is much more simply about looking, offers a moment of intimacy. At the same time she has begun to give life and independence to the dead meat of pornography.

This new concern to give her work its own breath and movement has led Wiltshire away from re-staging

HERMIONE WILTSHIRE
Seamen 1991, installation at Dreadnought Seamen's Hospital

pornographic imagery, which though sophisticated in subverting the mechanics of desire, could not achieve a new life of its own. An important stage in this development was the installation which Wiltshire originally intended for the Seamen's Mission, a disused hospital in Greenwich. In this, now titled 'Seamen', what look from afar like a spray of sparkling drops of clear water are seen, from above, to individually cover a photograph of a penis. The two images bring together cause and effect in one. The glass alternately conceals and reveals, attracting and repelling. Is this act private or public, over or not yet begun? The sex of both the protagonist, and an acknowledgement of that of the viewer suddenly becomes imperative. Are we implicated in this act or not? Are we part of its nexus of desire?

Wiltshire's most recent work no longer demands that the spectator acknowledge his or her gender, but now aims for a more complete restoration of the relationship with the body. She has mainly been engaged with finding ways of lifting the body off the page and into the material itself. One strategy has been to make the framing take on a life of its own, and she has used curved frames of wood or seemingly liquid plaster around specially commissioned domed or blown glass. She has effected the transition of the frame into the work, and into its meaning. The plaster supports of 'Two Points of Speech in Sight' suggest some kind of original matter, the original unformed. In the case of 'Puff' this base matter is given status by its gilding. These plaques puncture and give breath to the walls against which they are hung.

Glass is the traditional framer; it focuses and yet it distances. Wiltshire equates it with the screen, which again is both a barrier and a support, the boundary between real space and illusion. Wiltshire has followed-up other associations which glass brought with it. As it cools it wrinkles, and this led her into making the fingerprints of 'My Touch'. 'My Touch' deals with the literal mark or sign of the body, but the glass carries over, and because it acts like a magnifying glass, it also suggests the forensic associations of fingerprinting. Here Wiltshire has also been able to allow glass to reveal its natural qualities: adhesion, flexibility, brittleness. Its liquid sparkle attracts, its adhesive appearance implicates the body's presence. It seems both liquid and brittle; it is in the process of taking shape and yet has already snapped. We know glass is dangerous. 'My Touch' secures the spectators' position and then abandons them.

Alongside the material element of her work, Wiltshire continues to use photography. Though she wishes to revive photography's physical presence, she incorporates it almost as if it were the verbal or intellectual element of her works. The framing of the photographs at the centre of her sculptures suggests a nugget or kernel of information; it is the signifier which sets off the viewer's attempt to describe. At the centre of 'Two Points of Speech in Sight' is a pursed mouth. But the raised glass lens which protects the photo is like an unseeing eye, returning your gaze. It also suggests oral activity; blowing or breathing. Wiltshire confuses the mouth with the eye, speaking with seeing, silence with blindness.

Pauline Cummins and Louise Walsh

Pauline Cummins and Louise Walsh worked on 'Sounding the Depths' as a one-off collaboration. Normally they work separately; Cummins is known for the video work which she has made over the last decade, while Walsh has primarily worked in sculpture since graduating. However it is the political and religious shaping of the woman's situation in Ireland that was their shared point of concern, and it is against this background that 'Sounding the Depths' should be understood.

The collaboration arose out of an invitation to the Irish Women Artists Action Group to make a contribution to a meeting in Glasgow, but ended up with Cummins and Walsh taking forward motifs that they found worked well together. At that time Cummins had taken up the cockle – both the shell and the shellfish – to represent vulnerability and strength, and female sexuality, while Walsh was working on imagery of the mouth and what comes out of it. Pursuing this concern with the closed and open body and its vocalisation, Walsh was now interested in working with the voice. Thus their collaboration moved beyond some formal national contribution to a joint residency at the new Irish Museum of Modern Art.

To make a work that refers to women in Ireland almost inevitably involves acknowledging the suppression of Irish women's rights over their bodies. Despite this, both artists were determined to make a work which would posit the possibility of independence. The particular background to this work may well have promoted its extreme overtness. They used themselves as models, and, with the intention of referring both to society's mores and to its conventional modes of representation, decided to explore underneath the body's surfaces.

The phrase 'Sounding the Depths' refers to fisherman's soundings of the unknown depths below to see where the shoals lie. Sound is understood to be crucial; as sound locates the catch under the water, so sound gives the body its wholeness. The origins of the title lend associations to the unknown inner depths of the bodies - to fertility and riches - and to the soundings used in physiological examinations.

Cummins and Walsh's installation provides a sequential reading of space which is like a journey from the closed to the open, with associations shifting between the protected and the vulnerable. The image of the closed shell leads into a corridor at the end of which a video is projected; its visual and aural effect one of tension and lack of ease. The spectator then moves into a larger room where five over life-size images of female bodies look back from the walls. They are accompanied by a sound track of laughter, and the images themselves are at once surprised and triumphant.

The device by which Cummins and Walsh's photographs open up the body and give it a voice - so that it is at once subject and object - is simple but powerful. At first the imagery is shocking, as it looks like a wounding. It will also read as sexual, perhaps especially if one knows the Celtic image of the Sile na Gig, who wears her vagina on her stomach. However, a realisation of the sources of the super-imposition - the open mouth over the body - brings with it an understanding of less sensationalist meanings. The body is not invaded, instead it is represented as whole. There is even the sense that the body is asserting its wild will over its bearer, and we are left asking if the voice is the voice of reason, and where it finds its home? Thus, despite the very rawness of the piece, we are left with ambiguities; open and closed can be interchangeable, and though the body is open, it is able to resist meaning. Rather than leave us with the pious image of the whole woman, the work is dangerous enough to disturb both our readings and our expectations.

Endnote

Words are strikingly absent from *Elective Affinities*. Even here, with 'Sounding the Depths', where the voice does emerge out of the silence, it is not a voice which shapes words, but which laughs.

Our relationship to art always returns to our fundamental inability to describe it. The works on show here deal directly with this inarticulacy. They take art away from verbal description, and focus on our physical experience of standing in front of it. They are about not-speaking, but understanding through the body.

BATAILLE, THE BODY & CONTEMPORARY ART

Brian Crosskurth

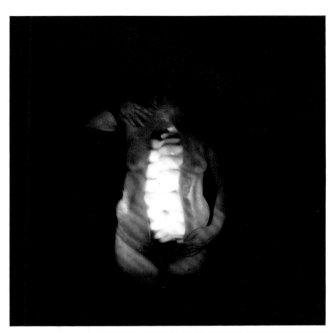

PAULINE CUMMINS AND LOUISE WALSH
Cibachrome print from *Sounding the Depths* 1992

In the summer of 1930, the French writer, Georges Bataille, embarked upon an examination of the human mouth. Gazing into its depths, he drew certain disconcerting and alarming conclusions. In an article published in the same year, he remarked that the savagery of the orifice in animals, its capacity to terrify, to maim, to kill, is retained in the human order, despite the refinements of civilization:

> ...the violent meaning of the mouth is conserved in a latent state...on important occasions human life is still bestially concentrated in the mouth: rage makes men grind their teeth, while terror and atrocious suffering turn the mouth into the organ of rending screams. On this subject, it is easy to observe that the overwhelmed individual throws back his head while frenetically stretching his neck in such a way that the mouth becomes, as much as possible, an extension of the spinal column, *in other words, in the position it normally occupies in the constitution of animals*. As if explosive impulses were to spurt directly out of the body through the mouth, in the form of screams. (Bataille, p.59)

Bataille argues that the violence of certain physical impulses demands this primal, screaming abyss in place of the cerebral brain as its outlet. The fragile mastery of the closed mouth, 'as beautiful as a safe', in contrast, is strictly human in damming up such intense disorder.

Bataille's striking imagery can be readily related to the work of Pauline Cummins and Louise Walsh. Enormous, livid mouths appear recurrently in their images, gaping, hissing, shrieking, breaking open the body and rupturing its unity. Where the viewer anticipates continuity and wholeness, a dark orifice cuts open the stomach and seems to speak from the shadowy figure.

Similarly, in confronting the oddly cropped limbs and strange physical displacements in the photographs of Hannah Villiger and Thomas Florschuetz, Bataille's writing on the body compellingly presents itself:

> The play of fantasies and fears, of human necessities and aberrations, is in fact such that fingers have come to signify useful action and firm character, the toes stupor and base idiocy... The hideously cadaverous and at the same time loud and proud appearance of the big toe corresponds to this derision and gives a very shrill expression to the disorder of the body, that product of the violent discord of the organs. (Bataille, p.22)

It would be possible to juxtapose such passages, in collage-like fashion, with the works in this exhibition. With its profusion of bizarre angles and unexpected perspectives, Bataille's writing can be aligned with the dislocations perpetrated by the eight artists gathered here. Yet his texts may also provide a grid through which to view these images by taking a preliminary detour through the work of another writer.

A child stands before a mirror, a luminous, reflective surface which he has indifferently crawled or tottered past many times before. Yet today something happens. A gesture of jubilant recognition punctuates the fascinated gaze which he fixes on his own image. He sees *himself* in the mirror.

This is the 'mirror stage' conceptualized by the French psychoanalyst, Jacques Lacan, as the initial phase in the formation of individual identity. Before the first recognition of the self in the mirror between the age of six and eighteen months, the infant experiences his body as fragmented and dispersed. In the gesture of identification, however, this uncoordinated sum of unwieldy limbs becomes realigned in an ideal self-image. In the mirror stage, the child anticipates an imaginary physical control which he has yet to attain. The narcissistically charged contours of the reflected body define a figure possessing unity, identity and mastery. In Lacan's view, the imaginary idealization of the body initially traced in the mirror stage marks a central dimension of the individual's subsequent experience of the self and of others. The body is marked out as a unified totality, complete and whole.

At this point, however, it is necessary to interrupt

Lacan with a third passage from Bataille:

> The vicissitudes of organs, the profusion of stomachs, larynxes and brains traversing innumerable animal species and individuals, carries the imagination along in an ebb and flow it does not willingly follow, due to a hatred of the still painfully perceptible frenzy of the bloody palpitations of the body. Man willingly imagines himself to be like Neptune, stilling his own waves with majesty; nevertheless, the bellowing waves of the viscera, in more or less incessant inflation and upheaval, brusquely put an end to his dignity. (Bataille, p.22)

Bataille's strategy here is to deploy the body as a vital, chaotic force countering the narcissistic illusion of mastery. Although the texts in which this movement is initially sketched out predate, by two years, Lacan's first published investigations of idealizing projection in the early 1930s, the analyst's thinking clarifies what is at stake in Bataille's writing. It is the mirage of control, unity and identity which the invocation of 'the bloody palpitations of the body' targets. It is this physiological chaos, this unpresentable fragmentation that is excluded from the false perfection of the mirror stage. And its return signals danger.

It is Bataille's stress on fragmentation, the excision of the eye, the severance of the toe, the isolation of the shrieking, bestial mouth from the reflective human visage that shatter the body's deceptively complete appearance. The proper identity of the human figure is violently disrupted by a relentless focus on forms whose startling dislocation renders them anonymous and strange.

At first glance, Bataille's preoccupations would seem to align him with Surrealism. Yet while there are certainly strong links connecting the writer with the panorama of dismemberment present in the art of Magritte, Dali and others, he was never a part of the movement itself. Indeed, Bataille was to be the object of intensely disparaging criticism in André Breton's *Second Surrealist Manifesto* of 1929. It was an attack that specifically involved questions of beauty and the body.

The immediate pretext for Breton's onslaught was Bataille's essay, *The Language of Flowers*. In this text, the writer asserts that the conventional symbolism and beauty ascribed to flowers collapses in the face of a darker, more disturbing face of things. Behind the ravishing loveliness of red rose petals, of blue hyacinths, of jewel-like tulips is a monstrous ugliness. Stripped of their seductive adornment, they display a stark hideousness which the eye can barely contemplate. In this naked state, Bataille argues, flowers bear a strange and disconcerting resemblance to genitalia in their evocation of the more obscure spaces of sexuality.

Inspired by his glimpse of an unpresentable horror, Bataille asks us to imagine what lies behind a calm and pastoral woodland scene. Beneath the lush green leaves and gently swaying branches, there is a repellent world of tangled roots and obscene tubers thrusting themselves into the blackness of the earth. It is hardly a vision to inspire a lyrical celebration of nature. This subterranean nightmare corrodes the idealizing vision which sees the rolling fields and woods irresistibly ascending to the heavens. In place of the elevated values of justice and rectitude allegorically imagined in such a scene, there is a hideous underground before which high ideals are difficult to sustain.

It was Bataille's final, arresting image, however, that especially aroused the Surrealist's anger. At the conclusion of his essay, Bataille evoked the Marquis de Sade, imprisoned in the insane asylum of Charenton, tearing the petals off the most dazzling roses and tossing them into a ditch of liquid manure. In this ignominious anecdote, he asserted, lay the revelation of beauty's ugly truth.

The Language of Flowers forms an integral part of Bataille's 'low materialism'. He opposed this current of thought to the disguised idealism that simply elevates the idea of matter to the position of the supreme principle of being. Far from challenging the religious outlook, Bataille argues, such a materialism merely shuffles its terms, substituting the notion of dead matter for that of God. At the same time, stable, inert matter provides a convenient alibi for science as the new religion. In rejecting this perspective, Bataille calls for a materialism that will exclude all idealism through its 'direct interpretation of raw phenomena' (Bataille, p.16). He expanded upon this formulation by stating that 'low matter' is foreign to ideal aspirations through its resistance to all philosophical systems. Rather than being limited and defined by reason, as is the case in an idealizing materialism, such baseness designates the very limits of rational thought as the domain of excess and exorbitance beyond its boundaries.

Bataille proposed that the study of this exorbitant space of 'low matter' be named 'heterology'. Amid the scattered unpublished papers in which he counterattacked the Surrealists in 1929, Bataille defines heterology as 'the science of what is wholly other' (Bataille, p.102). In negative terms, such strange terrain comprises elements that cannot be subordinated to utilitarian considerations. In this sphere of unproductive expenditure, he ranges forms of excess that cannot be contained within the limits of social and philosophical rationality: orgiastic sexuality, death, laughter, excrement and, somewhat curiously, solar energy which he sees as the epitome of such mad, useless spending.

Bataille's heterology did not fail to leave its imprint on his writings on art. In his studies on Van Gogh, he stressed the elements of the sun and sacrifice above all else. As the operation that subtracts the object from the space of the useful in order to devote it to the sacred, sacrifice also exemplifies unproductive expenditure. In the modern era, the sacrificial impulse can take on bizarre and idiosyncratic guises. For this reason, Bataille opens his first text on Van Gogh with a gruesome, documentary account of one Gaston F. who tore off his left index finger while staring fixedly at the sun. It was the solar rays, the young psychotic later explained, which had ordered him to commit this act of self-mutilation.

Such intertwining of sacrificial and solar themes will mark Bataille's vision of Van Gogh, for both the sun and sacrifice are crucial instances of unproductive expenditure. In this light, he sees the cutting of the ear and the obsession with sunflowers as intimately related. Both embody the unleashing of dangerous heterogeous forces. Behind the dazzling beauty of sunflowers, there lurks a brutal, unpresentable violence. As the representatives of unrestrained solar expenditure, Van Gogh's painted flowers mark out in advance the traumatic space which the artist's self-mutilating act will later occupy:

> ...one can doubt that even those who have ever torn and mutilated themselves amid screams and to the beat of a drum have abused this marvellous freedom to the same extent as Van Gogh, who carried his severed ear to the place that most offends polite society... The monstrous ear sent in its envelope...brusquely leaves the magic circle where the rites of liberation stupidly aborted. (Bataille, pp.70-71)

In *The Language of Flowers* and in *Sacrificial Mutilation and the Severed Ear of Van Gogh*, both natural and artistic beauty are related to a space of disturbing heterogeneity. Beauty, in this sense, is a gorgeous radiance that both reflects and masks a blinding otherness. Stared at directly, the sun obliterates the very source of vision. From Bataille's perspective, the dark materiality to which beauty is inseparably related is both its condition of possibility and the fatal limit at which its fragile loveliness shatters.

All of this is rather far from Surrealism. If the term is to be understood as designating the aspiration to fuse the imaginary and the real in the poetic spirit, then Bataille's emphasis on materiality strikes a distinctly discordant note. Indeed, Breton strenuously objected to the writer's 'low materialism'. For the Surrealist leader, beauty was to be found instead in the ideal atmosphere of the imagination, a homogeneous space of poetic purity. The body was excluded. It could be admitted into the Surrealist universe only once it had been transfigured through the vision of the spirit.

It is the materiality of the body above all else which links the artists in this exhibition to Bataille rather than to the Surrealism of Breton. Despite superficial similarities, their work displays an immediacy and directness that has little relation to the disembodied fantasies of Magritte and others.

Another writer attacked and banished by Breton, Antonin Artaud, focused with equal intensity on the body:

> a sharp burning sensation in the limbs, muscles twisted, as if flayed, the sense of being made of glass and breakable, a fear, a recoiling from movement and noise. An unconscious confusion in walking, gestures, movements... a state of painful numbness, a kind of numbness localized in the skin which does not inhibit any movement but which changes the internal sensation of a limb and gives the simple act of standing up straight the value of a victorious effort.

> Probably localized in the skin, but felt as the radical elimination of a limb, and presenting to the brain only images that are far away and not where they should be. A sort of internal fracturing of the whole nervous system. (Artaud, pp.64-65)

For both Artaud and Bataille, the body is the site of a radical dispossession. Limbs and sensations are unsettled in a general vortex of disorientation and, above all, the mind is not master of this odd house. But whereas Artaud feared and hated such effects with a violence reminiscent of *Dr. Strangelove*, Bataille assumed an unequivocally positive view. The expropriation of the ideal unity of the self through the dislocation of the human figure was an opening of multiple possibilities in his eyes. In negative terms, it also effectively undermined powerful ideologies which denigrate the lowly, material body on the basis of allegedly spiritual values:

> Although within the body blood flows in equal quantities from high to low and from low to high, there is a bias in favor of that which elevates itself, and human life is erroneously seen as an elevation. The division of the universe into subterranean hell and perfectly pure heaven is an indelible conception, mud and darkness being the principles of evil as light and celestial space are the principles of good: with their feet in the mud but their heads more or less in light, men obstinately imagine a tide that will permanently elevate them into pure space. Human life entails, in fact, the rage of seeing oneself as a back and forth movement from refuse to the ideal, and from the ideal to refuse — a rage that is easily directed against an organ as base as the foot. (Bataille, pp.20-21)

By shifting his focus to the 'low' features of the body, Bataille sought to break this entire hierarchy rather than simply to reverse its terms. Through dislocation and fragmentation, the body as a terrain of traditional ideological investment and power relations could be, in his view, irrevocably changed. Torn out of context, its contours become literally unrecognizable.

Such defamiliarization is a recurrent feature of the work in this exhibition. In Thomas Florschuetz's photographs, for example, the parts of the body are subjected to a sustained blurring of identity. The viewer is initially confused by these strangely isolated and juxta-

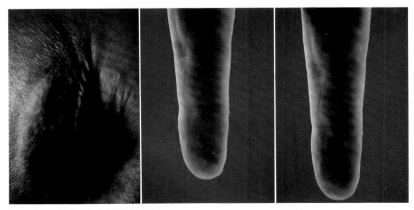

THOMAS FLORSCHUETZ
Untitled, triptych No 34 1992

posed fingers, eyes and feet. Cut off from the reassuringly familiar image of the complete figure, such fragments possess an uncanny charge.

A similar logic is encountered in the art of Hannah Villiger. Although the artist employs her own figure as the constant subject of her photographs, no ideal image of the self is presented in these works. Instead, contorted fragments of the body short-circuit and disorient the process of identification in several senses: the *subject* of the representation eludes immediate naming, while the viewer is unable to locate or project an ideal self-image in these powerful photographs.

Certain of Villiger's views of twisted, distorted feet recall Bataille's anthropological observations:

> Man's secret horror of his foot is one of the explanations for the tendency to conceal its length and form as much as possible ... this uneasiness is often confused with a sexual uneasiness ... the Chinese, who, after having atrophied the feet of women, situate them at the most excessive point of deviance... The same aberration is found among the Turks ... who consider it immoral to show their nude feet... [In Europe] modesty concerning feet developed excessively and only started to disappear in the nineteenth century... [In] Spain ... women's feet have been the object of the most dreaded anxiety and thus were the cause of crimes. (Bataille, p.21)

Bataille's comments underline the degree to which the historical mapping of the body into 'high' and 'low' areas has been determined by the politics of gender. While 'Man willingly imagines himself to be like Neptune, stilling his own waves with majesty', woman is linked with 'a hatred of...the bloody palpitations of the body' (Bataille, p.22). As a real living power rather than as an idealized form, the female body is designated as both a dominated and excluded zone of impurity. It is 'low' organic matter counterposed to the 'high' male head, sovereign and aloof in the rarefied domain of the spirit.

Many of the artists in the exhibition challenge this dominant ideology of gender. In such a context, the strategy of fragmentation works on a number of specific levels. First, it acts to achieve the well-known effect of refusing to display the woman as an object for the voyeuristic male look. On a somewhat less familiar level, the dislocation and disorientation of the figure highlights the female body as a vital and disruptive force in its own right. The imagery of contortion that has such sinister overtones in surrealist art with its echoes of actual violence against women, both past and present, is turned against itself. The traditional hierarchy of 'high' and 'low' is reversed and dismantled with an accompanying emphasis on excluded materiality. Louise Walsh and Pauline Cummins, Jayne Parker, Hannah Villiger and Hermione Wiltshire all deploy the fragmented figure to counter the mirage of unity, control and identity characteristic of Man's 'mirror stage'. In the case of Jana Sterbak's *Golem*, it is the ideal mastery of the imaginary masculine figure itself that is literally disconnected.

Helen Chadwick's work functions in a rather different way. Nevertheless, Bataille's texts on the body are equally if not more germane in this instance. The artist's fashioning of delicate, crystalline forms from the flow of urine strikingly recalls the writer's insistence that beauty springs from heterogeneous and unpresentable sources. One of the principal incarnations of the 'unproductive expenditure' that embodies beauty's precondition and extreme limit was, for Bataille, the body's wastes. In Chadwick's *Piss Flowers*, the streams of urine have shaped figures that suggest the very emblem of masculine power: the phallus. Yet through their vaguely amorphous fragility as well as their derivation from both a female and male origin, these forms are no longer governed by traditional symbolic conventions. Instead, they fracture such normative patterns in much the same way as Bataille's flowers. Indeed, the scandalized reaction of certain sections of the media to Chadwick's work underlines the degree to which the body can still represent a radically threatening force in contemporary art.

At first glance, there is nothing more identifiable and reassuringly familiar than one's 'own' body. Yet as Bataille's texts and the artists in this exhibition stress, the human figure can be more effectively seen as a disorienting space of otherness, an endless series of fragments whose unity is perpetually in question. The effect of such works is to interrupt the automatic responses of identification and projection: they introduce strangeness and unfamiliarity where a mirror image is anticipated. What emerges is an unsettling power, a force of interrogation which overshadows the pleasures of ideal reflection.

BIBLIOGRAPHY

Artaud, Antonin. *Antonin Artaud. Selected Writings,* ed. Susan Sontag, trans. Helen Weaver (New York: Farrar, Strauss and Giroux, 1976).

Bataille, Georges. *Visions of Excess. Selected Writings, 1927-1939,* ed. Allan Stoekl, trans. Allan Stoekl, Carl Lovitt, and Donald Leslie (Manchester: Manchester University Press, 1985).

Lacan, Jacques. *Ecrits. A Selection,* trans. Alan Sheridan (New York: W W Norton and Co., 1977).

LIST OF WORKS

Dimensions: height followed
by width (by depth) in millimetres

Page numbers refer to
illustrations of the works.

HELEN CHADWICK b.1953
Piss Flowers 1991-92
Bronze, enamel lacquer
Twelve bronzes, each c.1651 x 1575 x 1575
(pp48-51)
Collection of the artist
Helen Chadwick's 'Piss Flowers' were produced during an
artist's residency at the Banff Centre for the Arts, Alberta,
Canada. Financially assisted by the Canada Council's For-
eign Visiting Artist Programme, the Alberta Foundation for
the Arts and Angel Row Gallery, Nottingham

PAULINE CUMMINS b.1949 and
    LOUISE WALSH b.1963
Sounding the Depths 1992
A collaborative installation comprising five framed
Cibachrome prints, each 1845 x 1280 (pp62, 63), one
framed Cibachrome print 914 x 1016, one video
(stills pp60, 61) and one soundtrack

THOMAS FLORSCHUETZ b.1957
Refusal 1991
Cibachrome print
1800 x 1200 (p28)
The artist and Galerie vier, Berlin

THOMAS FLORSCHUETZ
Untitled Diptych No 61 1992
Cibachrome print
2 pieces, each 1800 x 1200 (p29)
The artist and Galerie vier, Berlin

THOMAS FLORSCHUETZ
Middle Segment 1993
Cibachrome print
1200 x 1800 (p30)
The artist and Galerie Nikolaus Sonne, Berlin

THOMAS FLORSCHUETZ
Curtain, 2 Pieces 1993
Cibachrome print
2 pieces, each 1200 x 1800 (p8)
The artist and Galerie Nikolaus Sonne, Berlin

THOMAS FLORSCHUETZ
The Emergence of Red Lines 1993
Cibachrome print
2 pieces, each 1800 x 1200 (p31)
The artist and Galerie Nikolaus Sonne, Berlin

JAYNE PARKER b.1957
K 1989
16mm film on video, 13 minutes (stills pp34, 35)
Collection of the artist

JAYNE PARKER
The Pool 1991
16mm film on video, 10 minutes (stills pp36, 37)
Collection of the artist

JAYNE PARKER
Cold Jazz 1993
16mm film on video, 17 minutes (stills pp38, 39)
British Film Institute Production

JAYNE PARKER
Cut Lengths 1993
Framed photograph
1190 x 1785
Collection of the artist

JAYNE PARKER
Untitled 1993
Framed black and white photograph
1190 x 1785
Collection of the artist

JAYNE PARKER
Le Bassin 1993
Framed black and white photographs
Three photographs measuring 530 x 710,
280 x 430, 530 x 710
Collection of the artist

JAYNE PARKER
Untitled 1993
Framed black and white photograph
550 x 900
Collection of the artist

JANA STERBAK b.1955
Golem: Objects as Sensations 1979-82
Seven lead hearts, bronze spleen painted red, lead
throat, bronze stomach, lead hand, bronze tongue,
lead penis, bronze ear, and three framed silver gelatin
prints each 328 x 243 (p9, pp42-44)
Installation size variable
Collection Musée des Beaux-Arts de Nantes

JANA STERBAK
I can hear you think (Dedicated to Stephen Hawking)
1984-85
Cast iron, copper wire, transformer, magnetic field,
and electrical cord. Head with electrical coil 130 x 88
x 110; other head 153 x 95 x 127; cord 3120 (p45)
Collection National Gallery of Canada

HANNAH VILLIGER b.1951
Sculptural 1984-85
Colour Polaroid mounted on aluminium
1250 x 1230 cm (cover, p22)
Collection of the artist

HANNAH VILLIGER
Sculptural 1984-85
Colour Polaroids mounted on aluminium
1250 x 7320 (p7)
Collection of the artist

HANNAH VILLIGER
Sculptural 1988-89
Colour Polaroid mounted on aluminium
1230 x 1250 (p23)
Collection Bächli/Hattan

HANNAH VILLIGER
Sculptural 1988-89
Colour Polaroid mounted on aluminium
1230 x 1250
Collection of the artist

HANNAH VILLIGER
Sculptural 1988-89
Colour Polaroid mounted on aluminium
1230 x 1250
Private Collection

HANNAH VILLIGER
Sculptural 1990-91
Colour Polaroid mounted on aluminium
1230 x 1250 mm
Collection of the artist

HANNAH VILLIGER
Sculptural 1990-91
Colour Polaroid mounted on aluminium
1230 x 1250 mm
Collection of the artist

HANNAH VILLIGER
Block XXII 1990
Colour Polaroids mounted on aluminium
2550 x 3790 (p24)
Kunsthaus Zug, Switzerland, Dauerleihgabe Kanton
Zug

HERMIONE WILTSHIRE b.1963
Puff 1993
Plaster and glass
800 x 800 x 400 approx (p55)
Collection of the artist

HERMIONE WILTSHIRE
My Touch 1993
Glass, Cibachrome prints, silicon glue
10 pieces, each c.150 x 100 x 35 (pp 56, 57)
Collection of the artist

HERMIONE WILTSHIRE
Two Points of Speech in Sight 1993
Plaster, glass and Cibachrome prints
Two pieces, each 500 x 500 x 100 (p54)
Collection of the artist

HERMIONE WILTSHIRE
Our Path 1993
Glass, Cibachrome prints, silicon glue
14 pieces, sizes various
Collection of the artist

HANNAH VILLIGER

HANNAH VILLIGER
Sculptural 1984-85

HANNAH VILLIGER
Sculptural 1988–89

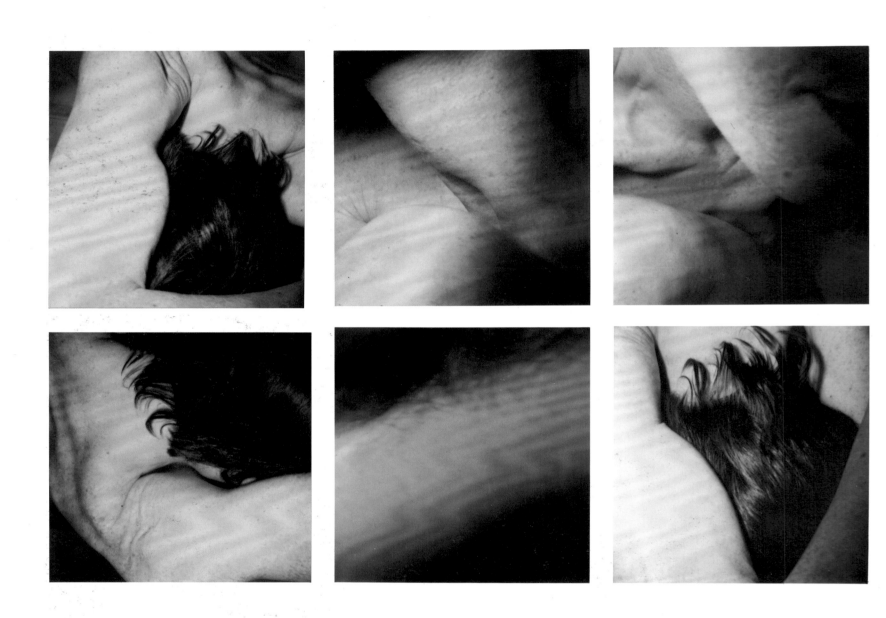

HANNAH VILLIGER
Block XXII 1990

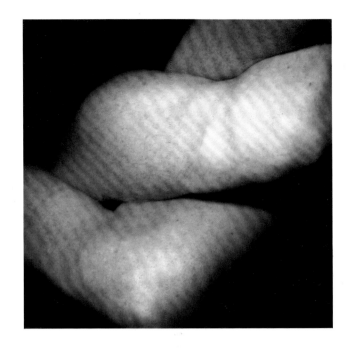

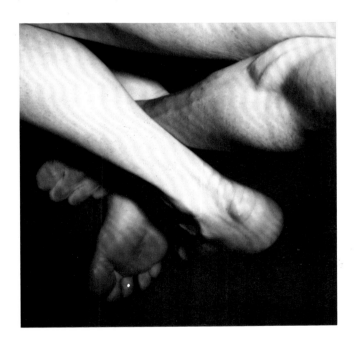

HANNAH VILLIGER
Work in progress 1993 (not in exhibition)

THOMAS FLORSCHUETZ

THOMAS FLORSCHUETZ
Refusal 1991

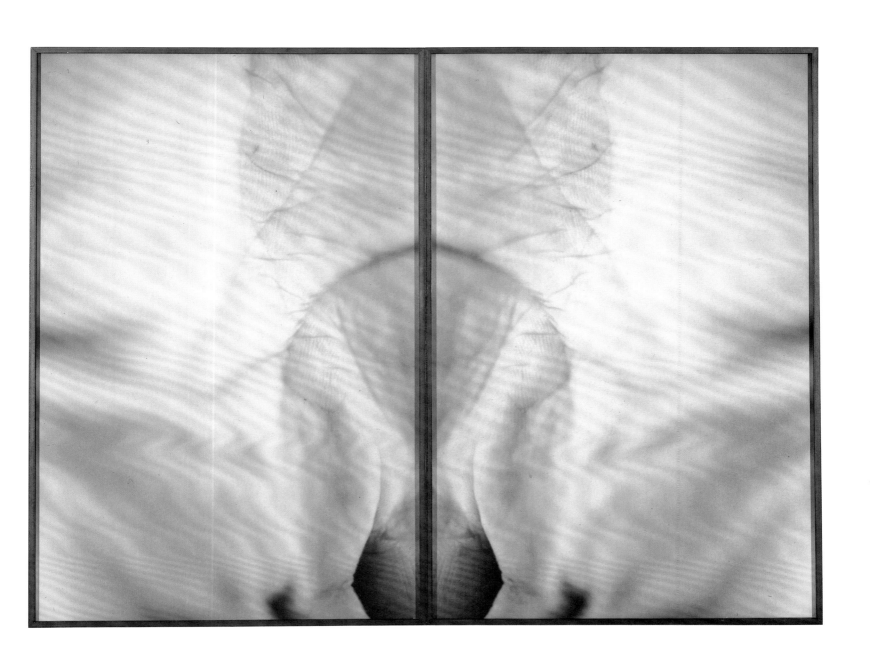

THOMAS FLORSCHUETZ
Untitled, diptych No 61 1992

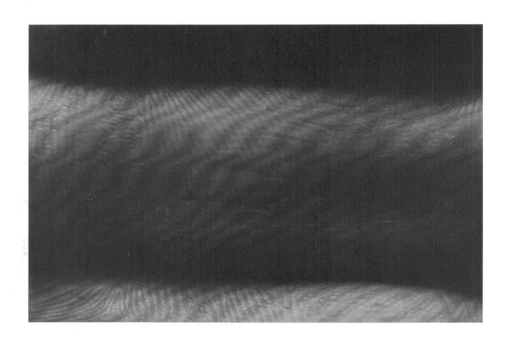

THOMAS FLORSCHUETZ
Middle Segment 1993

THOMAS FLORSCHUETZ
The Emergence of Red Lines 1993

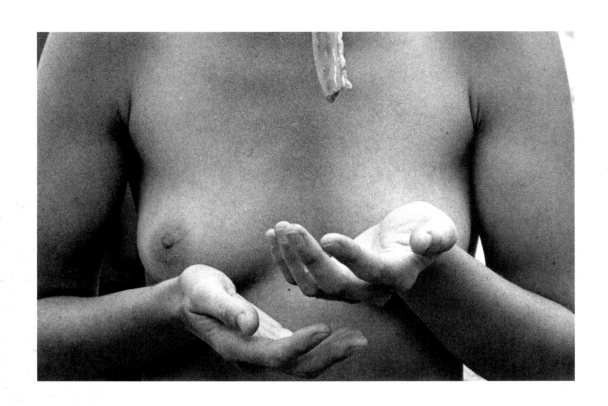

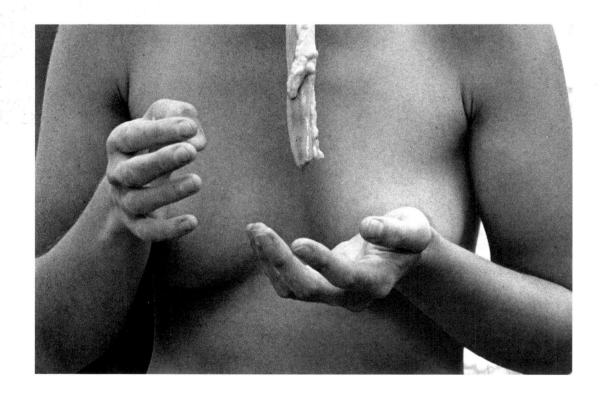

JAYNE PARKER
Film stills from *K* 1989

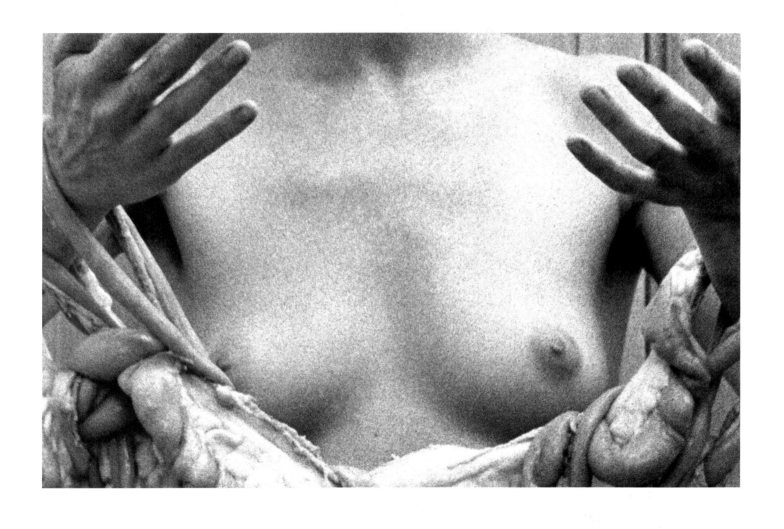

JAYNE PARKER
Film still from *K* 1989

35

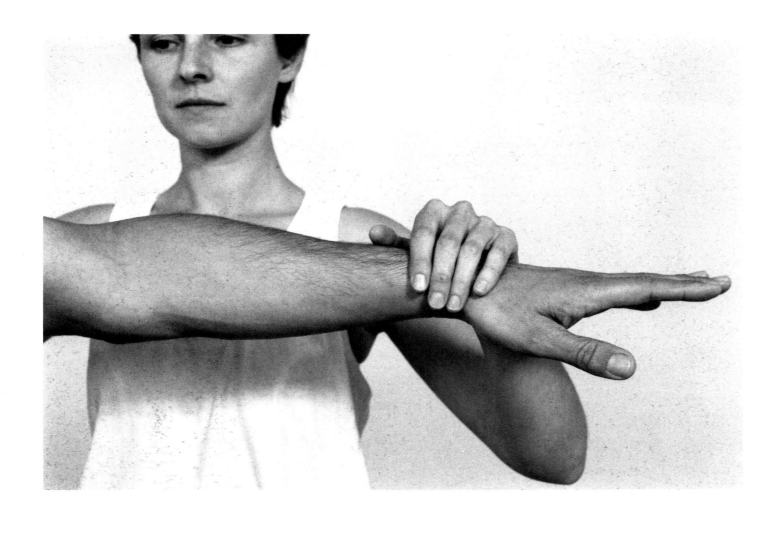

JAYNE PARKER
Film still from *The Pool* 1991

JAYNE PARKER
Film still from *The Pool* 1991

JAYNE PARKER
Film still from *Cold Jazz* 1993

JAYNE PARKER
Film still from *Cold Jazz* 1993

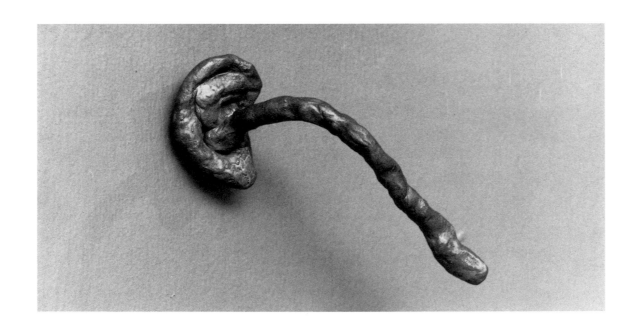

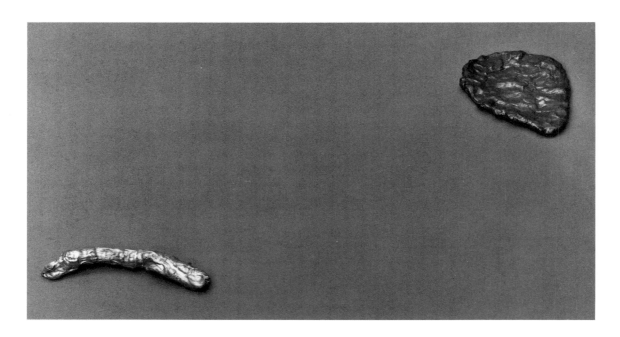

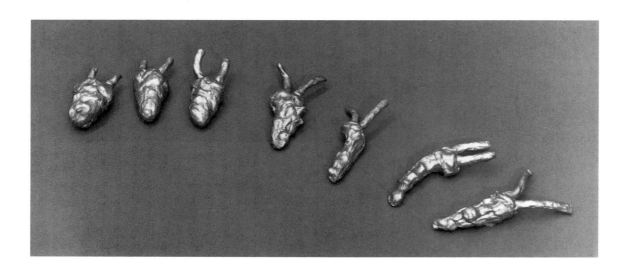

JANA STERBAK
Details from *Golem: Objects as Sensations* 1979–82
Bronze ear, bronze spleen and lead throat, seven lead hearts
opposite
Golem: Objects as Sensations, installation, Paris, 1992

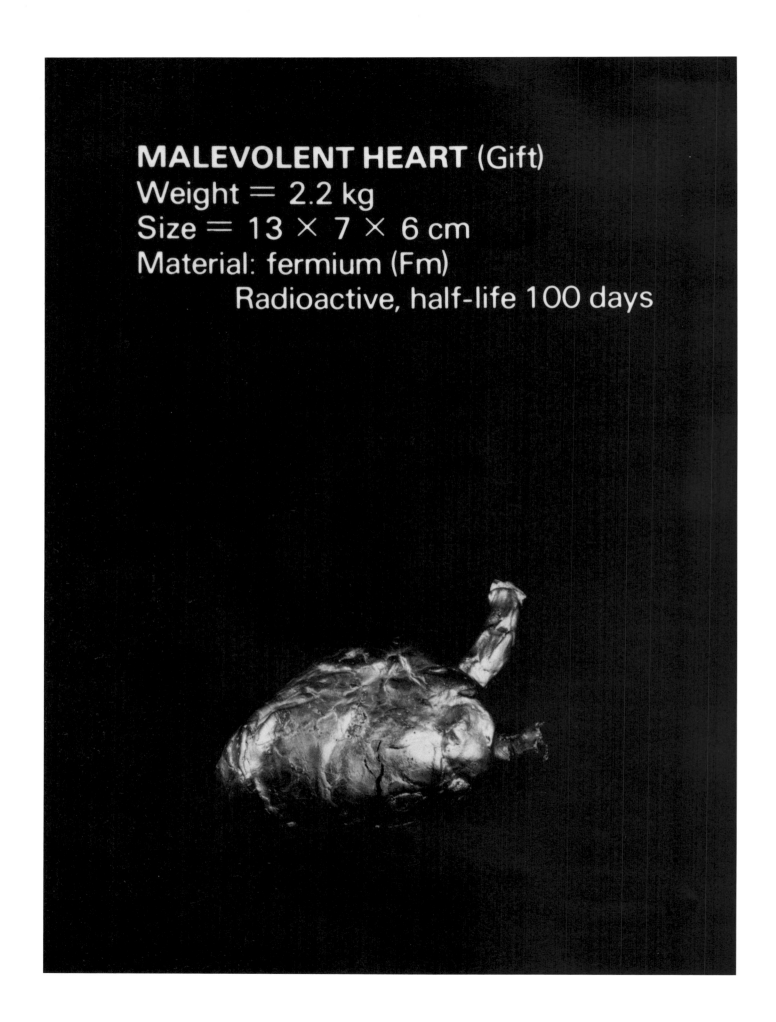

MALEVOLENT HEART (Gift)
Weight $=$ 2.2 kg
Size $=$ 13 $\times$ 7 $\times$ 6 cm
Material: fermium (Fm)
Radioactive, half-life 100 days

JANA STERBAK
Stomach (Venom), silver gelatin print 328 x 243, detail from *Golem: Objects as Sensations*

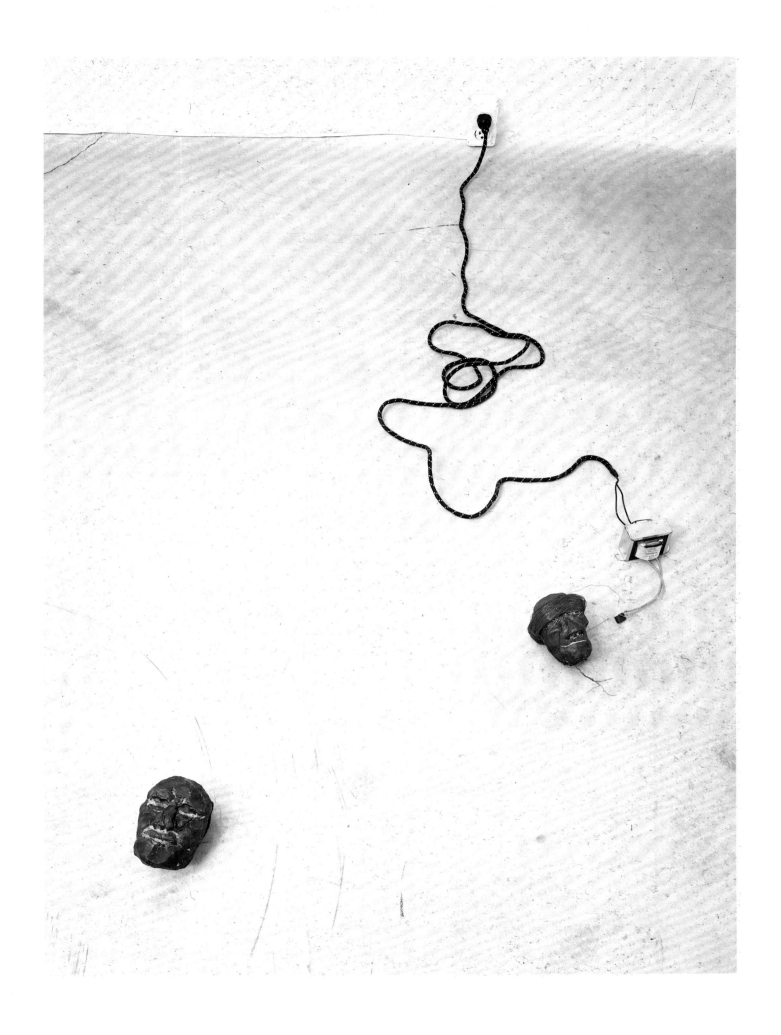

JANA STERBAK
I Can Hear You Think (Dedicated to Stephen Hawking) 1984–85

HELEN CHADWICK

PISS POSY

Drink me harder, my delight,
swell to bursting pretty sluice
and piss a posy
deeper, dear,
here – into my snow white

rain rogue about my pistil shot
hot juice, as if a bumblebee
would lick my petals,
pollinate me

for centre stage's a golden crown,
ring-a-ring a dandelion
molten amber
all falls down

calciferous, how Nature's art
does freeze our bold Indifference,
void now volume
daggled plume,
bespattered all around love's spume

locked together, you and I,
bind a hybrid daisy chain,
organs doubled
two a bed and
by a floral rhyming wed

Linnaeus what would you say,
how define such wanton play?
vaginal towers
with male skirt,
gender bending water sport?

each the other's measure wear
bared inside-up
contrariwise,
as if a chromosome could dare
to host such inverse pleasures, squared

Come sit on me, my mandrill's arse
cast priapic,
former fold,
suck my penis envy farce
like old Vénus de Lespugue

Helen Chadwick

HELEN CHADWICK
Piss Flowers Nos 3 and 8 1992

48

HELEN CHADWICK
Piss Flowers Nos 1 and 11 1992

HELEN CHADWICK
Piss Flower No 12 1992

HELEN CHADWICK
Piss Flowers, installation view, Nottingham, 1993

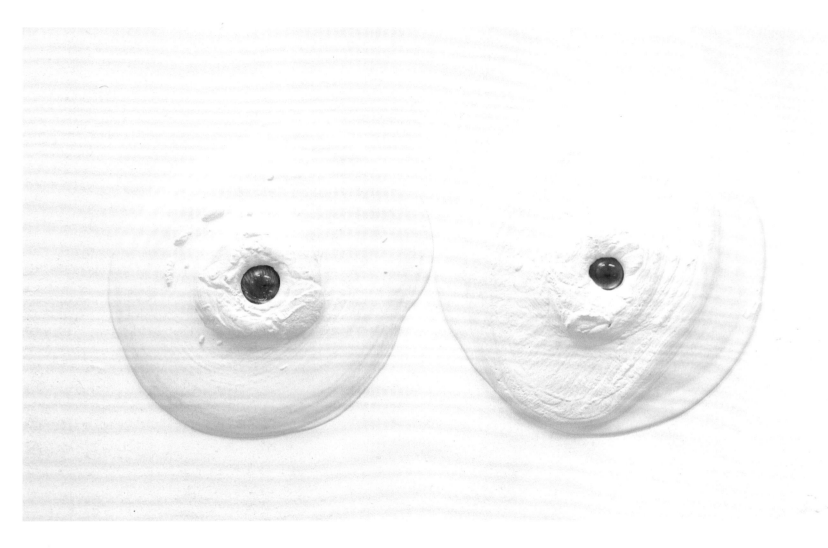

HERMIONE WILTSHIRE
Two Points of Speech in Sight 1993 and detail

HERMIONE WILTSHIRE
Puff 1993

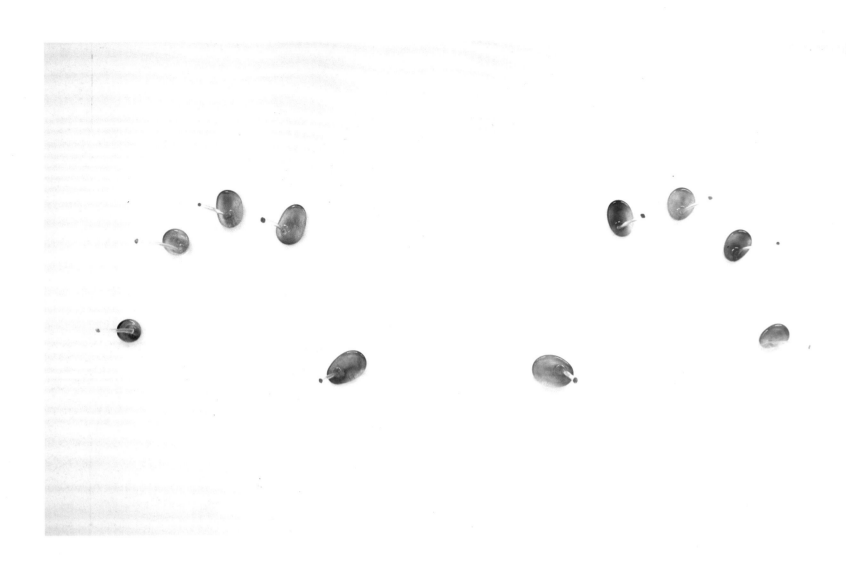

HERMIONE WILTSHIRE
My Touch 1993

PAULINE CUMMINS & LOUISE WALSH

PAULINE CUMMINS & LOUISE WALSH
Sounding the Depths 1992
Three-part collaborative installation. Details from the video above and opposite.

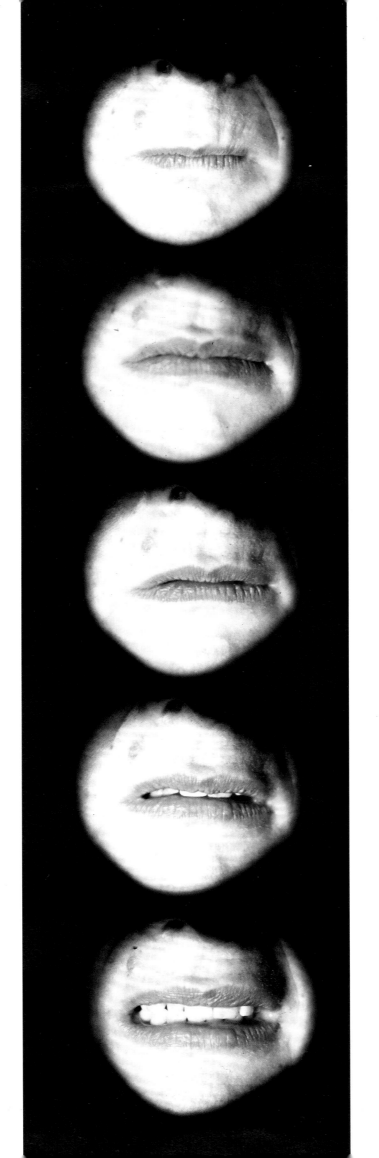

overleaf
PAULINE CUMMINS &
LOUISE WALSH
Sounding the Depths 1992
two of five Cibachrome prints
Running Woman, Whale Woman   61

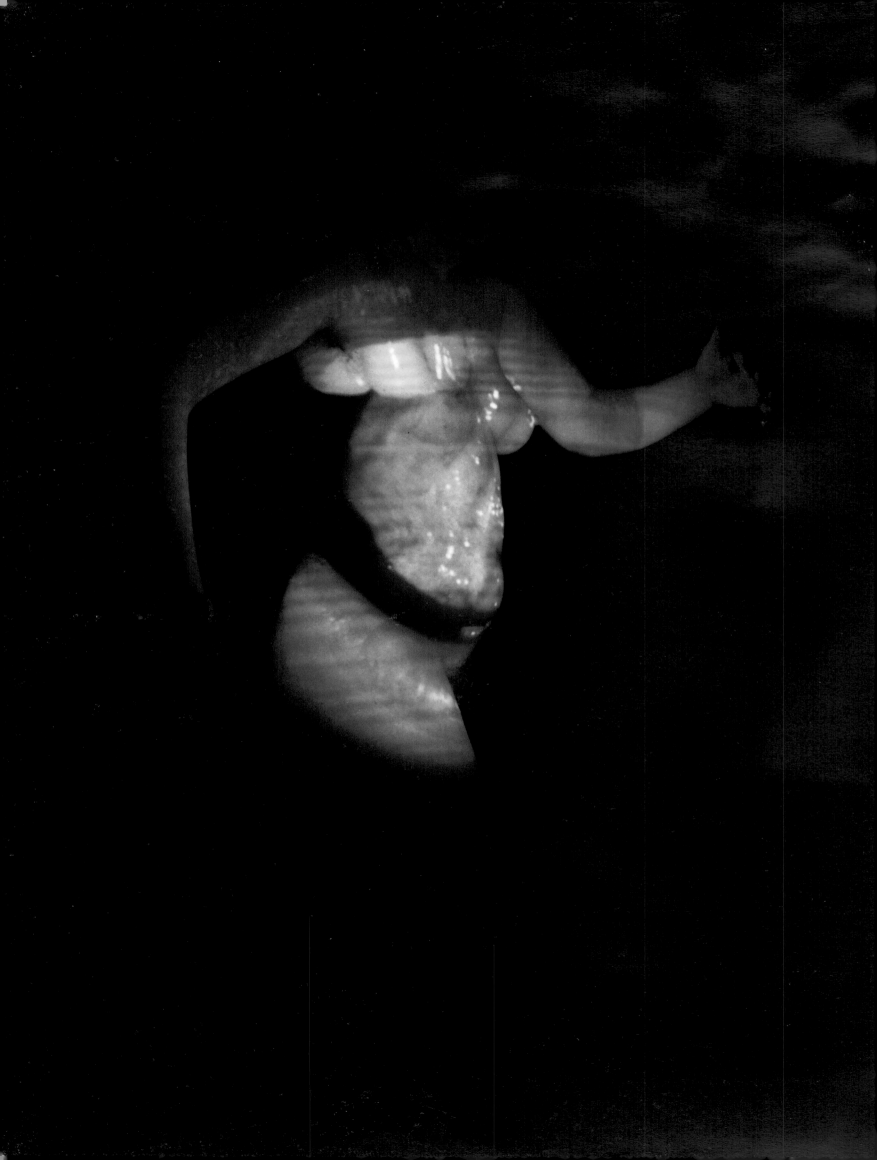

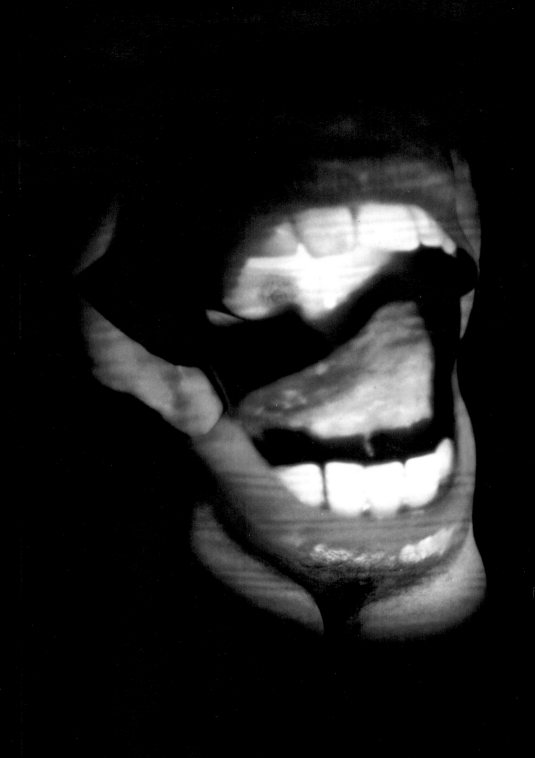

HELEN CHADWICK

Born Croydon, England, 1953
Brighton Polytechnic and Chelsea School of Art
1973-77
Living and working in London

One-person exhibitions

1978 *In the Kitchen*, Art Net, London
1978-79 *Train of Thought,* Acme Gallery, London and touring
1981-84 *Model Institution*, Newcastle Polytechnic and touring
1982 *Fine Art/Fine Ale*, Sheffield Polytechnic
1983 *Portraits Out of Placements*, Spectro Gallery, Newcastle
Growing Up, National Portrait Gallery, London; Cockpit Gallery, London
1983-85 *Ego Geometria Sum*, Art & Research Exchange, Belfast and touring
1986-87 *Of Mutability*, ICA, London and touring internationally★
1987 *Allegory of Misrule*, Birmingham City Museum & Art Gallery ★
Upon an Oval, Mappin Art Gallery, Sheffield
1988 *Cameos*, Torch Gallery, Amsterdam and touring★
Blood Hyphen, Clerkenwell Medical Mission, London (*Edge '88*)★
1989 *Lamps*, Marlene Eleini Gallery, London
Lumina, Portfolio Gallery, Edinburgh
Enfleshings, Interim Art, London
Viral Landscapes, Museum of Modern Art, Oxford and touring internationally
1990 *Meat Lamps*, Ehlers Caudill Gallery, Chicago and touring
1991 *Doubles*, Galerie d'Art Contemporain St. Vincent, Herblay (with Dany Leriche)★
In Side Up, Walter Phillips Gallery, Banff, Canada (with Shelagh Keeley); Mercer Union, Toronto★
De light, ICA, Philadelphia
Lofos Nymphon, Galerie Oboro, Montreal
1992 *Im Fleischgarten*, Friedman Guinness Gallery, Frankfurt; Produzentengalerie, Hamburg
Meat Lamps, The British School at Rome
Im Fleischgarten & Viral Landscapes, Galerie vier – Andreas Weiss, Berlin
1993 *Bronzes*, Angel Row Gallery, Nottingham

Group exhibitions

For group exhibitions up to 1989, see bibliography in:
1989 *Lifelines*, BASF, Ludwigshafen, Germany; Tate Gallery Liverpool★
The Thatcher Years, Flowers East, London
Triennale of Photography, Villa Merkel, Esslingen
Images of Women, Leeds City Museum & Art Gallery★
Fragments, The Gallery of Design, Merchandise Mart, Chicago★
1990 *Fotofest '90*, George R Brown Convention Center, Houston★
Paysage Demoralisé, Grey Art Gallery, New York

In Her Image, Barbara Toll Fine Arts, New York
The Journey, Usher Gallery, Lincoln
British Art Now: A Subjective View, Setagaya Museum, Tokyo and touring Japan
The Collector's Cabinet, Curt Marcus Gallery, New York
Images in Transition, National Museum of Modern Art, Kyoto and Tokyo
Withdrawal: Objects, Signs, Commodities, Forum Stadtpark, Graz
For the Wider World, British Council Touring Exhibition★
1991 *Real Fake*, Milan Rotunda; Villa Stuck, Munich
Long Live the New Flesh, Kettle's Yard, Cambridge★
De-Composition, Oriel Cardiff; and British Council tour in South America
Europa 1991, Badischer Kunstverein, Karlsruhe, Germany
Exploring the Unknown Self, Tokyo Metropolitan Museum of Photography
Le Corps Vacant, Musée d'Art Contemporain de Montréal
Postmodern Prints, Victoria & Albert Museum, London
Physical Relief, Hunter Galleries, Hunter College, New York
Les Couleurs de l'Argent, Musée de la Poste, Paris
1992 *Physical Encounter*, Gardner Centre, Sussex
Edge '92, London and Madrid ('Fruit Rage I and II')
37 Räume, Augustrasse, Berlin
Home, Kajaani Art Hall, Finland
Whitechapel Open, Whitechapel Art Gallery, London
Flora Photographica, Serpentine Gallery, London and touring
Traces of the Figure, City Museum & Art Gallery, Stoke on Trent; Cartwright Hall, Bradford
Innocence & Experience, City Art Galleries, Manchester and touring
The Boundary Rider, 9th Biennale of Sydney

PAULINE CUMMINS

Born Dublin, Ireland, 1949
National College of Art, Dublin, 1966-1970
Living and working in Co. Wicklow, Ireland

One-person exhibitions

1984 Kvindegalleriet, Aarhus, Denmark
1989 Gallerie Sct. Agnes, Roskilde, Denmark
1990 Ladengalerie, Munich
1993 *Sounding the Depths*, collaboration with Louise Walsh, Irish Museum of Modern Art, Dublin★

Group exhibitions

1982 *Celebration*, Tulfarris Art Gallery, Co. Wicklow
9 Months and After, Grapevine Arts Centre, Dublin
Irish Exhibition of Living Art, Carrolls Exhibition Centre, Dublin
1983 *Arts Week Exhibition*, Wexford Arts Centre
The Myth of Difference, Peacock Gallery, Dublin (with Rochelle Rubinstein)
1984 *Irish Exhibition of Living Art*, at Holles Street Hospital, Dublin
1985 *Neighbourhood Open Workshop*, Olympia Drive, Belfast
Old Wives Tales, Crescent Centre, Belfast
Illustrations from 'An tOllamh agus an Luchóg' (An Gúm, Dublin, 1981), touring Japan
Irish Exhibition of Living Art (with 'Inis t'Oirr'), Guinness Hop Store, Dublin
1986 *Eye to Eye – Irish Women Artists*, Women Artists Slide Library, Battersea Arts Centre, London
4 Women – 4 Cultures, Hunter College, New York
GPA Awards for Emerging Artists, Royal Hospital Kilmainham, Dublin
The School Show, Arts Council Touring Exhibition
1987 *Women's Caucus for Art*, National Conference, Boston, USA★
Visions – Women's World Congress Slide Exhibition, Project Arts Centre, Dublin
Women Artists Action Group Exhibition, (WAAG I), Guinness Hop Store, Dublin
Irish Women Artists, National Gallery of Ireland, and Douglas Hyde Gallery, Dublin★
1988 *New Work Newcastle '88*, (with 'Unearthed'), Projects UK, Newcastle-upon-Tyne
1989 *Art Beyond Barriers*, (WAAG II), Royal Hospital Kilmainham
Art Beyond Barriers, IAWA (International Association of Women in the Arts), Frauen Museum, Bonn★
ICTU Show, (Irish Congress of Trade Unions), Temple Bar, Dublin
1990 *Sexuality and Gender, A New Tradition – Irish Art in the Eighties*, Douglas Hyde Gallery, Dublin★
1991 *In a State*, Kilmainham Gaol, Dublin★
Inheritance and Transformation, Irish Museum of Modern Art, Dublin★
Available Resources, project with Orchard Gallery Derry, Northern Ireland
1993 *In Control*, Kunstlerhaus, Graz, Austria

THOMAS FLORSCHUETZ

Born Zwickau, East Germany, 1957
Living and working in West Berlin since 1988

One-person exhibitions

1987 *Hand im Herz*, Atelier Volker Heinze, East
    Berlin★
    Museum Folkwang, Essen
    Maison de la Roquette, Arles
    Galerie Neue Räume, West Berlin
1988 Galerie du Jour, Paris★
    Anderson Gallery, VCU, Richmond, Virginia★
1989 Aschenbach Galerie, Amsterdam
    P.P.S. Galerie F.C. Gundlach, Hamburg
    Montserrat Gallery, Montserrat College of Art,
    Beverly, Massachussetts
1990 Galerie du Jour, Paris★
    Grey Art Gallery, East Carolina University,
    Greenville, North Carolina
1991 Stadtgalerie Saarbrücken, Germany★
    L'Imagerie, Lannion
1992 Galerie vier, Berlin★
    Galerie Nikolaus Sonne, Berlin★
    Galerie du Jour, Paris★
    Galerie d'art contemporain dans l'Espace Jules
    Verne, Brétigny-sur-Orge, France★
1993 Forum Stadtpark, Graz, Austria
    Galerie Nikolaus Sonne, Berlin
    Goethe-House, New York

Group exhibitions

1987 *Out of Eastern Europe: Private Photography*, List
    Visual Art Center, MIT, Cambridge,
    Massachussetts★
    Preis für junge europäische Fotografie, Frankfurter
    Kunstverein
1988 *Figur & Zeichen*, Staatliche Kunstsammlungen
    Cottbus, Germany★
    Young European Photographers, Houston Foto Fest
    '88, Houston, Texas
    Small Scale, Rosa Esman Gallery, New York
1989 *Das Medium der Fotografie ist berechtigt, Denkaustösse
    zu geben*, Hamburger Kunstverein, Hamburg★
    Das Portrait in der zeitgenössischen Photographie,
    Kulturfabrik Mainz, Germany★
    Photographie als Kunst – Kunst als Photographie,
    Berlinische Galerie im Martin-Gropius-Bau,
    Berlin
    1 Internationale Foto-Triennale, Esslingen,
    Germany★
    New Photography V, Museum of Modern Art,
    New York
    Self and Shadow, Burdon Gallery, New York★
1990 *Berliner Kunststücke*, Sammlung der Berlinischen
    Galerie im Museum der Bildenden Künste,
    Leipzig★
    Jetzt Berlin! Malmö Konsthall★
    The Big Picture, San Francisco Museum of
    Modern Art
    Un couteau dans la photo, Galerie du Jour, Paris★
1991 *Salon Découverte*, Grand Palais, Paris

De ordine rerum, Palazzo delle esposizioni, Rome★
Interferenzen – Kunst aus Westberlin von 1960-1990,
Arsenal, Riga; Manege, Leningrad★
*Berlin! - The Berlinische Galerie Art Collection Visits
Dublin*, The Hugh Lane Municipal Gallery of
Modern Art, Dublin★
Galerie Vincenz Sala, Berlin
*Surgence - la création photographique contemporaine en
Allemagne*, Comédie de Reims, France and
touring★
Renta-Preis '91, Kunsthalle Nürnberg in der
Norishalle★
Bremer Kunstpreis '91, Kunsthalle Bremen★
Zone D - Innenraum, Leipziger Galerie für zeit
genössische Kunst★
1991/92 *Double Mentality*, Sezon Museum of Art,
Tokyo and touring in Japan
1992 *INTERFACE*, Corcoran Gallery of Art,
Washington DC★
Laboratorium photographicum, Berlinische Galerie
im Martin-Gropius-Bau, Berlin★
Echtzeit-Positionen deutscher Kunst, National
Museum of Contemporary Art, Oslo
Sprung in die Zeit, Berlinische Galerie im Martin-
Gropius-Bau, Berlin★
Ostdeutsche Fotografie von 1949-1989, Berlinische
Galerie im Martin-Gropius-Bau, Berlin★
Première photo, Galerie du Jour, Paris★
1993 *Berlin Art Scene*, Hong Kong Museum of Art and
National Museum and Art Gallery, Singapore★
Fontanelle, Landeskunsthalle, Potsdam★
Das Bild des Körpers, Frankfurter Kunstverein★
Anonymity and Identity, Anderson Gallery, VCU,
Richmond, Virginia★

JAYNE PARKER

Born Nottingham, England, 1957
Canterbury College of Art and Slade School of Fine Art
1977-82
Living and working in London

Screenings/exhibitions

1980 *Imagination is the Venom...* Ikon Gallery,
    Birmingham
1982 *Women Live* Festival, National Film Theatre,
    London
    Sense and Sensibility, Midland Group Gallery,
    Nottingham
1984 Cambridge Darkroom Season
1984-85 *The British Art Show*★, touring
1985 *Surrealist Traces*, Film and Video Umbrella, Arts
    Council touring show
    The New Pluralism, British Film and Video, Tate
    Gallery, London
1986 *Charting Time*, artists' notes for film and video,
    Serpentine Gallery, London★
    Light Years, London Film-makers Co-op, Rio
    Cinema, London
1987 *British Experimental Film*, Budapest
    The Animation Festival, Bristol
1987-1990 *The Elusive Sign, British Film and Video
    1977-87*, Arts Council show, touring abroad★
1988 *British Film Programme*, Moscow
    First International Film Forum, Riga, Latvia
1989 *Video Positive '89*, International Video Festival,
    Liverpool★
    The Body in Extremis, Film and Video Umbrella,
    launched at ICA, London and touring
1990 *Metaphors, Monologues and Landscapes*, Film and
    Video Umbrella, launched at ICA, London and
    touring
    London Film Festival, NFT, London
    Metaphorical Journeys, touring in America
    Between Imagination and Reality, ICA Biennal of
    Independent Film and Video, launched at ICA,
    London and touring★
    Arsenal, International Film Forum (retrospective),
    Riga, Latvia
    Sign of the Times, Museum of Modern Art,
    Oxford, and touring to Leeds 1991 and Marne-la-
    Vallée 1993★
1991 *11th Norwich Women's Film Weekend*
    Georges Bataille, An International Conference,
    Architectural Association, London
    Osnabruck Film Festival
    British Heretics, NFT, London
    25 Years of British Avant-garde Film-making, Tate
    Gallery, London
    Celluloid Bodies: Women's Film & Video, ICA,
    London
    Seventh Fringe Film and Video Festival, Edinburgh
    Film House
    Exiled: A Cinema of Shattering Truths, Film and
    Video Umbrella, launched at ICA, London and
    touring

1992 *Rotterdam Film Festival*
Driving the Loop, New British Film-makers, Tate Gallery, London
Erotica Creative, Vienna
Experimenta Festival, Museum of Art, Sydney
Arrows of Desire, The Second ICA Biennal of Independent Film and Video, toured internationally by the British Council★
1993 *Re-mapping the Female Body*, Tate Gallery, London
Brussels Film Festival
Innovation '93, The First Manchester International Film Forum

JANA STERBAK

Born Prague, Czechoslovakia, 1955
Vancouver School of Art; University of British Columbia, Vancouver; Concordia University, Montreal; University of Toronto 1973-1982
Living and working in Montreal

One-person exhibitions

1978 Pumps Art, Vancouver
1980 YYZ, Toronto
Travaux récents, galerie Optica, Montreal
1981 *How Things Stand Up*, Main Exit, Vancouver
1982 *Golem – Objects as Sensations*, Mercer Union, Toronto
1985 The Ydessa Gallery, Toronto
1987 The Ydessa Gallery, Toronto
Galerie René Blouin, Montreal
1988 The Power Plant, Toronto★
1989 The Western Front, Vancouver
Mackenzie Art Gallery, Regina★
Galerie René Blouin, Montreal
1990 Donald Young Gallery, Chicago
The New Museum of Contemporary Art, New York★
1991 *Jana Sterbak: Sisyphe II*, Galerie René Blouin, Montreal
Jana Sterbak: States of Being/Corps à Corps, National Gallery of Canada, Ottawa and touring in Canada and USA★
1992 *Projects 38*, Museum of Modern Art, New York★
Galerie Crousel-Robelin/BAMA, Paris
1993 *Jana Sterbak*, Louisiana, Museum of Modern Art, Humlebaek, Denmark★
I Want You to Feel the Way I Do, Fundacio 'la Caixa', Barcelona★
Jana Sterbak: Lénine rapetissé, Galerie René Blouin, Montreal

Group exhibitions

For details of group exhibitions from 1978-1989, see the exhibition catalogue for:
1989 *Canadian Biennal of Contemporary Art*, National Gallery of Canada, Ottawa★
1990 Donald Young Gallery, Chicago
TSWA Four Cities Project, Newcastle-upon-Tyne★
Galerie René Blouin, Montréal
Figuring the Body, Boston Museum of Fine Arts, Boston
Aperto '90, Venice Biennale★
Diagnosis, Art Gallery of York University, North York, Ontario★
1991 *The Wealth of Nations*, Centre for Contemporary Art, Ujazdowski Castle, Varsovie, Poland★
Un-Natural Traces, Contemporary Art from Canada, Barbican Art Gallery, London★
Interiors, Galerie Crousel-Robelin/BAMA, Paris
Un archipel de désirs: les artistes du Québec et la scène internationale, Musée du Québec★
With this ring..., Ikon Gallery, Birmingham★
Donald Young Gallery, Chicago

En hommage à un cadeau d'Eva Hesse à Sol Lewitt, Axe Néo-7, Hull, Quebec
The Embodied Viewer, Glenbow Museum, Calgary★
Vanitas, Galerie Crousel-Robelin/BAMA, Paris
1992 *GENERIQUE 1: DESORDRES*, Galerie nationale du Jeu du Paume, Paris★
Third International Istanbul Biennale
Marian Goodman Gallery, New York
Between the Sheets, P.P.O.W., New York
Internationale Kunstlerplakate, Saarbrucken, Germany★
Power Play, Betty Rymer Gallery, School of the Art Institute of Chicago★
Donald Young Gallery, Seattle
1993 *Destruction*, Munich
Fall from Fashion, Aldrich Museum of Contemporary Art, Ridgefield, Connecticut
Canada, une nouvelle génération, FRAC des Pays de la Loire, Garenne Lemot
Just to name a few, Barbara Weiss Gallery, Berlin
At the Edge of Chaos - New Images of the World, Louisiana, Museum of Modern Art, Humlebaek, Denmark
Clothing as Metaphor, Art Museum, Florida International University, Miami

HANNAH VILLIGER

Born Cham, Switzerland, 1951
Schule für Gestaltung, Zürich, and Schule für
Gestaltung, Lucerne, 1971-74
Living and working in Paris since 1986

One-person exhibitions

1982 Hogart Galleries, Sydney
1985 Galerie Lydia Megert, Bern
    Kunsthalle Basel★
    Galerie Susan Wyss, Zürich
1986 Centre Culturel Suisse, Paris★
1987 Zabriskie, Paris and New York
    Galerie Susan Wyss, Zürich
1988 Galerie Filiale und Peter Bläuer, Basel
1989 Museum für Gegenwartskunst, Basel★
    Zabriskie, Paris
    Musée des Beaux-Arts, Calais
1990 Zabriskie, New York
1991 Kunstverein Frankfurt
    Galerie Francesca Pia, Bern
    Kunsthaus Zug★
1993 *Midi-Minuit*, Cabinet des Estampes, Geneva★
    Galerie Filiale, Basel

Group exhibitions

1980 *Spektrum 80*, Galerie Rägeboge, Lucerne
    4.1., Aargauer Kunsthaus, Aarau, Switzerland★
1981 *Hammer II*, Basel★
    Aspekte der Jungen Schweizer Kunst, Städtische
    Galerie, Regensburg, Germany★
    Künstler aus Basel, Kunsthalle Basel★
1983 *Übersicht*, Aargauer Kunsthaus, Aarau★
1987 *Auf dem Rücken des Tigers*, Shedalle, Zürich★
    Offenes Ende - Junge Schweizer Kunst, Nuremberg★
    A choice, Kunst RAI 87, Amsterdam★
    *Stiller Nachmittag, Aspekte der Jungen Schweizer
    Kunst*, Kunsthaus Zürich★
1988 *Farbe bekennen, Zeitgenössische Kunst aus Basler
    Privatbesitz*, Museum für Gegenwartskunst, Basel★
1989 *Bilderstreit, Widerspruch, Einheit und Fragment in der
    Kunst seit 1960*, Rheinhallen der Kölner Messe,
    Cologne★
1990 *Le Choix des Femmes, Le Consortium*, FRAC,
    Nouvelle Usine, Dijon★
    Wichtige Bilder, Museum für Gestaltung, Zürich★
    Biennale Photographique, Centre de la Vieille
    Charité, Marseille★
1992 *Skulpturen - Fragmente, International Fotoarbeiten der
    90er Jahre*, Secession, Vienna★
    *Frammenti, Interface, Intervalli, Paradigmi della
    frammentazione nell'arte svizzera*, Museo d'arte
    contemporanea di Villa Groce, Genoa★
1993 *Toyama Now 1993*, The Museum of Modern Art,
    Toyama, Japan

LOUISE WALSH

Born Cork, Ireland, 1963
Crawford Municipal School of Art, Cork and
University of Ulster 1981-86
Living and working in Dublin

One-person exhibitions

1987 *On the Go*, Temple Bar Gallery, Dublin
    Otter Gallery, Belfast
1988 Arts Council Gallery Window, Belfast
1990 Arts Council Gallery, Belfast (with Alice Maher)
1992 *Sounding the Depths*, collaboration with Pauline
    Cummins, Irish Museum of Modern Art, Dublin★
1993 *Monument to the Unknown Woman Worker*, Great
    Victoria Street, Belfast (commission)

Group Exhibitions

1986 Royal Ulster Academy, Belfast
    Nicholas Treadwell Gallery, Canterbury, Kent
    Self Direct, Smith's Gallery, London
1987 *On the Go*, Temple Bar Gallery, Dublin
    Recent Works, Crawford Municipal Gallery, Cork
    Women Artists in Ireland 1970-87, Douglas Hyde
    Gallery, Dublin★
    Women Artists Action Group Exhibition, (WAAG I),
    Guinness Hop Store, Dublin
    Identities (Northern Irish Women Artists Group)
    Art and Research Exchange, Belfast
1988 *Sculpture Open*, Royal Hibernian Gallagher
    Gallery, Dublin
    Show N' Tell Gallery, San Francisco
    Fort Mason Fine House Gallery, San Francisco
    GPA Emerging Artists Exhibition, Douglas Hyde
    Gallery, Dublin
1989 *The Family*, Irish Life Mall, Dublin
1989-90 *Issues*, Arts Council of Northern Ireland, and
    touring★
1991 *In a State*, Kilmainham Gaol, Dublin★
    Available Resources, project with Orchard Gallery,
    Derry, Northern Ireland
1993 *In Control*, Kunstlerhaus, Graz, Austria

HERMIONE WILTSHIRE

Born London, England, 1963
Winchester School of Art; Central School of Art &
Design, London and Chelsea School of Art, London
1981-1987
Living and working in London

One-person exhibitions

1987 *Naym No Body*, Riverside Studios, London
1991 London, Riverside Studios (with Laura Ford)
1992 Lisson Gallery, London (with Richard Deacon)

Group exhibitions

1984 *New Contemporaries*, ICA, London
1985 *85 Degree Show*, Serpentine Gallery, London
1985-86 *Walking & Falling*, Plymouth Art Centre and
    touring
1987 *New British Art Show*, Air Gallery, London
    New Acquisitions, Fabian Carlsson, London
    The Artist Selects, Goldsmith's Gallery, London
1991 *Addressing the Forbidden*, Brighton Festival and
    Stills Gallery, Edinburgh
1992 *Traces of the Figure*, City Museum & Art Gallery,
    Stoke on Trent and Cartwright Hall, Bradford
1993 *What She Wants*, Impressions Gallery, York and
    touring
    Itself, Transmission Gallery, Glasgow

POSTSCRIPT ON GOETHE'S *ELECTIVE AFFINITIES*

Daria Santini

The title of Goethe's novel *Elective Affinities* (*Die Wahlverwandtschaften*, 1808-9) refers to a well known 18th-century scientific tradition in which the breakdown caused by the attraction between chemical elements leads to the construction of new compounds as if by free choice. While the chemists had employed a term related to human choice ('elective') to describe a natural phenomenon, Goethe uses the analogy in reverse and links human relationships to chemical affinities in his story of two couples whose irresistible cross-attraction recalls a chemical equation.

In the fourth chapter of *Elective Affinities* – which provides the actual framework of the text – one of the characters unwittingly anticipates the tragic events which will follow while at the same time explaining the meaning of the title:

> these cases are in fact the most significant and noteworthy of all; in them one can actually demonstrate attraction and relatedness, this as it were crosswise parting and uniting: where four entities, previously joined together in two pairs, are brought into contact, abandon their previous union, and join together afresh. In this relinquishment and seizing, in this fleeing and seeking, one really can believe one is witnessing a higher determination; one credits such entities with a species of will and choice, and regards the technical term 'elective affinities' as entirely justified[1].

Goethe borrowed the concept of 'elective affinities' and the idea of chemical attraction as an 'ethical symbol'[2] from the Swedish chemist Torben Olof Bergman, whose study *De attractionibus electivis* had been published in 1775 and translated into German ten years later; but his main sources came from other chemical and alchemical texts[3] that he knew from his own scientific research. However, given that Goethe always maintained the necessary link between the natural and the human/social sphere, the sources of *Elective Affinities* are both scientific and philosophical. Thus the novel's scientific references show that specific human matters are all part of a greater universal design.

It is in fact commonplace in eighteenth-century philosophy to find that natural and spiritual worlds are in some ways related. A good example of this – and a clear antecedent of Goethe's understanding of 'elective affinities' – is Johann Gottfried Herder's so-called *Spinoza Gespräche* (*Spinoza Dialogues*, 1787), where the discoveries of contemporary chemistry about the energy of inanimate bodies are similarly applied to human behaviour and emotions. Herder uses some examples that are very close to the ones Goethe employs in his novel and even mentions the scientific term 'Wahlanziehung' ('elective attraction') in order to define the inevitable magnetism between kindred individuals.

This notion however must also be connected to the ancient doctrine of sympathy, a term which was originally interpreted by the Greeks as a kind of friendship, as a deep affinity or even as a cosmic and almost magical power of attraction between similar people. Sympathy as an explanation for love is later to be found in the tradition of literary enlightenment, as for instance in Rousseau's novel *La nouvelle Héloise* (1761) where, like in Goethe's text, the laws of natural affinities lead to extramarital attraction. But while Rousseau represents these ideas in an enlightened, rational way and in the end brings about a conciliation between his characters and the ethical necessity of marriage, Goethe shows a more romantic, and tragic, concept of sympathy, so that the characters in *Elective Affinities* cannot help being overwhelmed by the inevitable natural rule of mutual attraction.

Although it is possible to trace some of the sources behind this work and one could try to give a more or less logical definition of its title as Goethe might have intended it, *Elective Affinities* remains one of the most elusive and mysterious novels ever written: its highly symbolic style, the intricacy of its motifs and the secret links often concealed behind them[4] make it, as Walter Benjamin said, a 'mythical phantasmagoria'[5] whose profound ambiguity is already stated in its contradictory title. The concept of 'elective affinities' is in fact a paradoxical one, as impulses ('affinities') are supposed to be natural, necessary and thus divorced from the possibility of free choice ('election').

In choosing this title Goethe aimed on the one hand

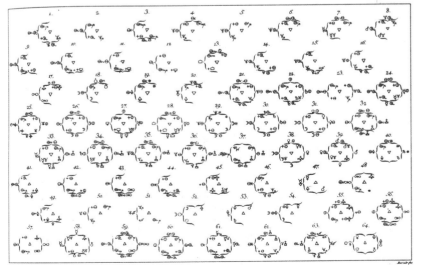

T O Bergman, symbolic diagram of 'Elective Affinities', 1783

to illustrate the tragic polarity between freedom of will and natural determination. However, the extreme complexity of the narrative leaves the reader with little certainty as to whether the characters have any choice at all or whether they are not rather impelled by an obscure and uncontrollable natural force. Thus the title is an effective metaphor for the irony and ambiguity which Goethe often used in his late work as an aesthetic criterion and which does not allow precise definition. Nevertheless, the concept of 'elective affinities' as Goethe meant it mainly symbolizes the ideas of the fundamental analogy between man and nature and of the mystery of human attraction. As he told his secretary Eckermann on the 7 October 1827:

> We all have something of electrical and magnetic forces in us and like the magnet itself, exercise a power of attraction and repulsion, according to whether we come into contact with something like or unlike ourselves.

NOTES

1. J W Goethe, *Elective Affinities*, translated by R J Hoolingdale, Penguin Books, 1971, p.55
2. J Adler, *'Eine fast magische Anziehungskraft'. Goethes 'Wahlverwandtschaften' und die Chemie seiner Zeit*, München, Beck, 1987, p.33
3. About the scientific sources of *Elective Affinities* see especially J Adler (cited), and A G Steer Jr, *Goethe's Elective Affinities. The Robe of Nessus*, Heidelberg, Carl Winter, 1990, pp.37-49
4. Goethe himself wrote in a letter to his friend Zelter on the 1 July 1809 that he had 'hidden many things in the text'.
5. W Benjamin *Goethes Wahlverwandtschaften*, Frankfurt a.M., Inselbücherei, 1964, p.25

opposite
First frontispiece of the *Aurea Catena Homeri*, published anonymously in 1723, one of the alchemical texts read by Goethe during his convalescence of 1768-69.

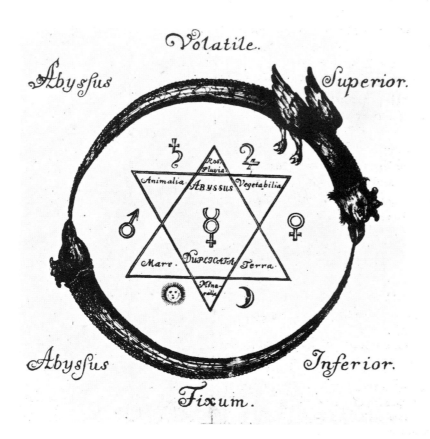